My Own Guru

My Own Guru

REZZAN HUSSEY

THOUGHT
CATALOG
Books

BROOKLYN, NY

THOUGHT
CATALOG
Books

Cover photography by ©Roksolana Zasiadko and Nick West, designed by KJ Parish.

Published by Thought Catalog Books, a publishing house owned by The Thought & Expression Co., Williamsburg, Brooklyn.

First edition, 2018

ISBN: 978-1945796043

Printed and bound in the United States.

10 9 8 7 6 5 4 3 2 1

For BB. For encouraging me to write.

CONTENTS

Foreword   1

Part I. Self-Knowledge Why Give A Damn?

1. How We Got Here   11
2. The Problems That Self-Knowledge Solves   19
3. The Road Ahead   31

Part II. The Reality Red Pills

4. Red Pill #1: Mindfulness   39
5. Red Pill #2: Responsibility   51
6. Red Pill #3: Acceptance   63

Part III. The Self-Knowledge Muscles

7. The Into the Woods Muscle   77
8. The Just Say No Muscle   89
9. The Roy Walker Muscle   99
10. The #NoFilter Muscle   103
11. The IDK Muscle   105
12. The Let it Go Muscle   111
13. The Eye of the Tiger Muscle   119
14. The Christian Grey Muscle   123

Part IV. You've Got a Big Ego (So Does Everyone)

15. Scoping Out the Self-Construct   135
16. WTF is the Hidden Self?   141
17. How to Use the Enneagram   149
18. Other Models: Attachment Theory, Myers-Briggs and   157
    Signature Strengths

Part V. The Real Slim Shady

19. The Emerging States of Self-Knowledge   169
20. Wider Benefits of Self-Discovery   181

Epilogue   183
About the Author   185
You Might Also Like...   187
Explore our world...   189

Foreword

The former UK Prime Minister, Benjamin Disraeli, said, "The best way to learn about a subject is to write a book about it."

That is why I started writing this book. One of the reasons, anyway.

The subject of this book is how to know yourself—a process sometimes called 'self-discovery'. This pursuit isn't fluffy and self-indulgent as people often imagine. In fact, and as this book suggests (more insists actually), self-knowledge is a prerequisite for a sane and happy life.

But knowing yourself is uncomfortable work. It takes a lot of effort before the chirpy crescendo of the Jimmy Cliff song, "I Can See Clearly Now" erupts like a volcano from inside you.

Not impossible though, I have learned.

It had taken me thirty-three years to stop sleep-walking my way through my life. The process set out in this book represents a roadmap of that journey, which I wrote partly to hardwire it into me, and partly to spare you the time and trouble.

So why the focus on self-knowledge?

It wasn't a conscious decision to focus on it, but the link between self-knowledge and happiness has been demonstrated to me repeatedly over the last three years. Here's the story:

On 1 January 2015 and at the onset of a new chapter in my life, I was on a plane to Thailand (one-way ticket, of course. It wouldn't be much of a story otherwise.)

I hadn't been through a separation like Liz Gilbert before she went to *Eat Pray Love*. I wasn't grieving like Cheryl Strayed before she took off for her walk on the *Wild* side. I wasn't even still all twitchy from insecurity like I had been during my twenties.

Actually, nothing particularly interesting had happened for a while in my life. I was restless. I went to Thailand because it was there and because I was fortunate in that I could.

Back then, I took little joy in my work (I edit legal journals by profession), but loved the freedom of being a freelancer. I was a year or so out of a serious relationship, and all that dating seemed to be teaching me was how little I knew about what I wanted and needed in a romantic partner. I was just using people, I guess, like we all do when we haven't yet figured out what we are doing: to validate our beliefs about ourselves and love.

I stayed for nine months in Thailand, mostly in Chiang Mai—northern Thailand's largest city.

I don't really know what I thought would happen after I transferred my life to Thailand. I know that I did not expect, around the middle of my stay, to start dating a cute Australian guy and start a blog with this guy and his brother. Being a blogger or a writer hadn't been in my aspirations. Some other unexpected stuff happened that year too.

When I returned to stay at my mum's place in London in September 2015, I noticed some major shifts in my perspectives—valuable ones. It's the same for a lot of us who go away and come back, isn't it?

But it wasn't long before I slipped back into feeling restless again. Although I had found something I enjoyed doing (writing), I didn't know what the point of it was, or even if there needed to be a point.

My relationship with the cute Aussie had ended after I got back to London. The experience had left me saddened and more determined than ever to develop my understanding of what I wanted and needed in a romantic partnership.

So a little after New Year in January 2016, I was on a flight to Cancun in Mexico, my destination being Playa del Carmen. I stayed for six months, and more interesting stuff happened, some of which I'll tell you about if you stick around. In July, I was faced with a decision: should I go back to London now? I just wasn't sure.

I considered various locations and settled on New York. I had always dreamed of living in New York.

I stayed for six weeks with a sixty-year-old former model whose room in on the Upper West Side I rented relatively affordably. I lived a pretty artsy six weeks mostly reading, writing and walking through Central Park. From New York, I made a detour to Detroit to visit a friend I had made whilst in Mexico. I flew back to London just in the nick of time for Mum's big birthday bash.

That was August 2016. In September, I started working on this book. It was called 'Know Yourself' back then.

Since then, the travel has slowed down. I've made trips away from London, but they've been shorter in duration. Most of the time, I feel like I could be anywhere and I'd be reasonably happy and content.

And I don't feel restless anymore.

———————

I am 90% sure I wouldn't have written this book—and perhaps anything—had I not travelled to Thailand when I did.

But long before I was writing about personal development, I

was pursuing it like a crazed beast, reading everything I could and attending courses. And honestly, what was driving that was dissatisfaction. Looking back, I can see I was completely out of touch with myself. I was isolated from the guru.

It is said that a person's true expertise will probably be in an area where they are the most troubled. My trouble has been in knowing what I truly want to do and who I want to be. And in the immortal words of Sam Smith: I know I'm not the only one.

There is literally a world of information out there for anyone seeking answers to questions regarding fulfillment, happiness and self-realisation. My own quest led me to explore many different self-improvement teachings from across psychology, philosophy, and spirituality. And a lot of it has the potential to be life-changing when applied.

But personally, I have found it challenging to avoid using personal growth material like I've used other things: as a way to stay fascinated rather than to implement. There is a gulf between knowing and being, and in that gap lies our freedom.

And so we get to another reason I wrote this book: to inspire you to commit in a radical way to your growth and (metaphorical) expansion, instead of only bothering to water the plants when they are dying. As my friend Jeff once said, "Being happy is not easy." It's true. We have to work for it every single day through the medium of our little decisions.

I don't know what your motivations are for reading this book—whether you are feeling just curious or you are on the brink of despair (hopefully more the former).

I do know that if you ever feel like you can't seem to get your shit together, or that you have no idea what you are doing with your life, you can stand to learn something about the person you truly are.

I think that deep down, we all want to realise our full potentials. For me, trying to do that involved a lot of weird decisions and painful self-experimentation. However, I have come to internalise the maxim that life happens for us rather than to us. In other words, if something is happening, then it isn't wrong. We are all being constantly challenged to grow into a larger, more awesome version of who we are.

Knowing yourself better really does bear remarkable fruits. For instance, now I know the true meaning of emotional self-reliance; not the kind where you're avoiding people for fear of being hurt. I can create my own happiness and contentment on demand. I've basically reclaimed my power—the power I did not know I had given away. I have become my own guru, and I believe that anyone can by changing the way they pay attention.

I hope by now you have a clearer picture of the person writing to you. Now let's have a closer look at this thing called self-knowledge and awareness to see if it's for you.

Time, in other words, for the carrots.

Part 1

Self-Knowledge
Why Give A Damn?

When I discover who I am, I'll be free.

— Ralph Ellison, Invisible Man

1

How We Got Here

Before we look at the troubles with not knowing ourselves, I wanted to provide a bit relevant context about how we have tended to approach the work of self-discovery to date. Hopefully, you won't find it too dull.

Self-knowledge was man's original homework assignment. It was the Athenian philosopher, Socrates, who assigned it when he said "know yourself," although he didn't say how to do it (bad Socrates).

Several solutions have been offered over the years, among them 'Self-Awareness Theory' developed by the psychologists Duval and Wicklund in the 1970s. Duval and Wicklund said that when we "focus our attention on ourselves, we are able to evaluate and compare our current behaviour to our internal standards and values, and that this is what elicits a state of objective self-awareness."

Later on another psychologist, Daniel Goleman, said self-awareness was "knowing one's internal states, preferences, resources and intuitions." Dan said the trick was to recognize your own emotions and how they affect your thoughts and behaviour.

Focus your attention on yourself. Know your internal states.
Should be simple, given that we are around ourselves all the time. Right?

Wrong!

So why is it such a ball-ache?

We Don't Care

Firstly and most obviously, we just don't value self-insight as a thing worth having.

Were you ever encouraged to explore how your childhood continues to shape you? Or to learn of the main ways you go about getting your needs met (these are just examples)?

Unless you have ever spent time in therapy, I am guessing not, which is odd considering that getting the answers to these questions makes a tangible difference to the quality of our lives.

It has taken me a long time to accept this, but some of us just don't value self-analysis even as we run into issues in adulthood. Given that you have bought a copy of this book, unless I coerced you into doing so, then I can imagine you have decided that self-knowledge is kind of important.

Lack of Priority

So we might realise that self-knowledge is important, but just don't see it as being that important. This was the category that I personally was in for a long time. This mindset is a product of a Western environment.

In the West, we are more concerned about advancement and achievement than insight and awareness, and so we tend to work hard on the things in life that make us look or even feel good temporarily. Our appearances and careers take precedence over things such as insight and reflection. This is a mistake.

The fall-outs that can happen as a result are well documented. Have you ever seen the documentary, *Minimalism: A Documentary About the Important Things*? Watch it and you'll know what I'm talking about.

We Avoid Introspection

So what if we do value self-knowledge enough to devote some time to it? We must still overcome a sizeable challenge.

We do not gather self-knowledge exclusively through the conventional route of learning anything—reading and education. We also gather insights through reflecting on our experiences and by paying attention in the moment as we move through our lives. Often, this route is neglected for various reasons. This is especially the case for those who would categorise themselves as 'extroverts'.

The practices set out in this book acknowledge the various methods through which we develop self-knowledge. My belief based on my experience is that without a combination of them all, our self-discovery efforts only take us to a certain point.

The Mind Lies

In one of his many moments of lucidity, the writer George Orwell said: "To see what is under one's nose needs a constant struggle."

The reality is that often, we wouldn't know the truth if it

sidled up to us and did the smelliest fart ever. Our minds are wired to keep us in the dark. And an undirected mind is:

1. Drawn to negativity.
2. Reactive.
3. Essentially a product of the ultimate of all deceivers: the ego.

I don't want to go techie about the nature of the mind so early in our journey together as we are going to delve deeper into it.

Briefly, modern psychology tells us that the mind goes on autopilot mode when it can. Most of us are on autopilot at least half of the time.

Due to the way our brains evolved, autopilot is the equivalent of operating in survival mode. That means that, left to our own devices, our thoughts are like magnets for whatever the perceived anxious, stressful or fearful event of the day or hour is. They say that around 80% of our thoughts have negative content.

Coupled with that, the subconscious side of the mind isn't an easy beast to know. Despite this—and as anyone who has ever tried and failed to resist their favourite vice is aware—humans are primarily irrational beings. We are dictated by feelings and emotional responses.

The third point requires further insights from psychology. We now know that we develop our egos, also called self-constructs, from an early age as a way to cope with childhood. After a while, we may forget that we were anything other than this ego or self-construct. And unless we try to observe it objectively, we may not ever free of ourselves from its dysfunctional aspects. And everyone's self-construct has dysfunctional aspects.

Observing ourselves objectively not only requires learning new skills for a lot of us but also battling with some natural impulses. One of these is our 'Freudian resistance' to our negative aspects. Another is our desire for immediate gratification. You get the picture. Orwell was right: it's hard to see yourself clearly.

Mass Self-Deceptions

In addition to the lies of the mind, there are the lies that characterise a lot of our thinking. I call them universal self-deceptions because they are very common ways of thinking.

One such deception is that we aren't in control of our perspectives—that other people and events exert influence over our mood and happiness. This one seems to be tacitly accepted by most people.

It's Getting Harder

There are modern affronts to knowing ourselves—challenges that earlier generations didn't have (theirs were different).

The author Jonathan Fields summarised this well when he said that we have a self-knowledge crisis on our hands, and that "the problem isn't that we don't have the answers. We've had them for thousands of years. It's that the things that work are either engulfed in a vast sea of noise or offered in a way that doesn't land."

The crux of it is that our discernment skills haven't kept pace with technology and the explosion of information. Our attention is always outside, and we are slowly losing the ability for introspection and internal referencing.

Blogger and author Mark Manson says: "We've all had those days or weeks (or months or years) where we've felt scatter-brained—out of control of our own reality, constantly sucked down rabbit holes of pointless information and drama comprised of endless clicks and notifications. To be happy and healthy, we need to feel as though we are in control of ourselves and we are utilizing our abilities and talents effectively. To do that, we must be in control of our attention."

It isn't just self-knowledge that suffers. In his book *Deep Work*, Cal Newport argues that the ability to focus deeply on a single project, idea or task for long periods of time is the most important skill for becoming successful in our time.

Force of Inertia

The power of inertia—the tendency to do nothing or to remain unchanged—fixes us all in place at times.

I think that the major thing that has helped me with mine is travel. This perhaps explains why travel seems to be a key element of a lot of self-discovery stories.

The British/Swiss author Alain de Botton has written that: "Travel can—when approached in the right way—play a critical role in helping us to evolve; it can correct the imbalances and immaturities of our nature, open our eyes, restore perspective and function as the most meaningful agent of maturation. We should aim for locations in the outer world that can push us towards where we need to go within." It's an idea that resonates with me a lot.

You don't need to travel to fend off inertia, and you may not be able to right now. But we all need to ensure that we resist it somehow. Inertia is a powerful counterforce to pretty much anything good.

2

The Problems That Self-Knowledge Solves

I'm not going to make trumped-up promises regarding the results of knowing yourself. What I am suggesting to you is that the practices in this book will shift your emotional landscape significantly to a more positive, empowered place.

My own attitudes have changed so drastically that I barely recognise myself from my late twenties (I'm in my mid-thirties now). True, inner changes do create outer changes as your attitudes inform your actions. But I really encourage you to keep the focus internal.

Here are eight specific challenges that knowing yourself better helps with:

1. Doing unfulfilling work and a lack of success.
2. Being powerless to break habits.
3. Insecurity in dating and relationships.
4. Being addicted to chasing external validation.
5. Low self-esteem.
6. Not knowing what you want.
7. Lacking a sense of purpose.
8. Feeling like happiness is somewhere just ahead.

Doing Unfulfilling Work and a Lack of Success

In addition to helping us to become successful in a conventional sense, greater self-knowledge can literally move the goalposts on how we see success. That's because ultimately, only a values-led sort of success is satisfying in the long run. And values-led success relies on… guess what? Knowing your values.

In the West, we tend to lead a goal-focused life with success defined in terms of status, wealth and power. Typically, we aren't so closely connected with our values.

During our teens, we love thinking about what we will do and who we will become, but life sucks us up to standardised activities. "The mass of men lead lives of quiet desperation and go to the grave with the song still in them," said Thoreau in *Walden*. It's sad but true.

At the time I chose my graduate degree (law), I didn't know what the hell I wanted to do or if I would be good at. I just did something that seemed sensible. That became a problem much later on in my mid-twenties when I realised I didn't really enjoy working in law, nor was I particularly good at it.

We don't have to do work that we love all the time, and all jobs have their tedious elements. But given that most of us spend a large proportion of our lives working, we have to stop kidding ourselves that enjoyment isn't a factor at all.

I used to tell myself my work didn't matter and that fulfillment could be found in other streams. I have since changed my position on that. I think it does matter—quite a lot.

I also used to tell myself that conventional success, such as making loads of money, wasn't important to me. I still kind of think that, but I would say now that one product of 'self-actualisation' (or realising your potential) is a visible recognition of how your life contributes to others. And in the world we live in, recognition comes in the form of financial reward.

A person who is fulfilled in their work and successful doing what they do is:

- Achieving great things in their chosen field.
- Being rewarded for doing so either financially, or through recognition, or ideally both.
- Heavily drawing on their specific talents and skills.
- Enjoying their work.

Preceding that happy pinnacle, we have the person who is:

- Financial rewarded, but unhappy and unfulfilled by their work.
- Fulfilled, but barely earning enough to get by.
- In the words of the immortal Morty of *Ricky and Morty*, an agent of average: the person who is hitting mediocrity in terms of what they are doing, how they are being rewarded and how they feel about it.

There is a story behind each of these scenarios: a set of beliefs, a behaviour pattern. A story that self-knowledge helps us to see.

Defeated by Negative Habits

Being trapped repeatedly by self-defeating behaviour is depressing. I've been there. There are various factors that affect our capacity to change our lives. Self-knowledge is how we come to know our own obstacles.

Many of us fall prey to the power of procrastination after setting goals. And we assume that's because we are lazy and incapable of managing our time. But in reality, procrastination is usually fuelled by feelings of nameless anxiety which we can overcome with greater awareness.

When the problem isn't procrastination, it might appear to be a lack of willpower, which is another human condition we fail to understand. Exercising self-control is often pitched as a battle between the cruder self, driven by pleasure, and the aspirational self, driven by deeper wants.

But what becomes clear when you delve deeper into habit change is that the most powerful self is the emotional self. As we already looked at, this side of us is difficult to know.

Developing our self-knowledge helps us to know this emotional self. If we are able to accurately decipher what's driving us in real time, we are more likely to be able to make better choices.

We also tend to have no idea about the role of non-acceptance, for example, in our failure to change our habits. The link between acceptance and habit change is something we'll return to in Part 2.

Relationship Angst

For me, developing my self-understanding has been the single biggest investment I have made in my relationship happiness. It's so important.

How does the person with self-knowledge behave in their romantic lives?

The largest impact for me has been on my confidence and security. With self-knowledge naturally comes self-love and self-acceptance, and from there you are just in a much stronger position to deal with whatever you encounter.

There are a few other things that self-knowledge has helped me with:

- Enjoying the experience of dating for what it is.
- Having a clearer sense of what type of person compliments me.
- Taking things less personally.
- Dealing with rejection better.
- Not becoming infatuated.
- Not attaching expectations to things.
- Taking responsibility for my emotions.
- Improving confidence in communicating my needs.
- Not using people for distraction or entertainment.

I think when we don't know ourselves well enough, among other things we:

- 'Ride our results' in dating (i.e. only enjoy it if things are going well).
- Project insecurities and read situations wrongly.
- Are needy without realising it.
- Take things personally.
- Blame our partners for upsetting us.
- Remain unaware of how to get our needs met inside of a relationship.
- Enter into second-rate relationships because we are scared to be alone.

Now I love a good theory, and in the area of relationships, there are some hugely helpful ones out there. In Part 4, we will look at one of them: Attachment Theory.

Even without the aid of a theory, committing to self-observation in relationships takes us a long way in improving the quality of relationships. Also, the same practices that help us to know ourselves (e.g. mindfulness, a Part 2 practice) help us to manage the difficult emotions that being in close relationship with someone else presents.

Caring Too Much About What Other People Think

The Chinese philosopher and writer Lao Tzu said: "Care about other people's approval and you become their prisoner." It's bang on.

I do not believe we should aspire to reach a stage where we don't give a toss what people think about us. I do, however, support the idea of caring a lot less.

Being externally validating has multiple consequences across life. When the focus of our attention is external rather than internal, we might:

- Be highly susceptible to social comparison and insecurity.
- Fall prey to jealousy and envy, which can cause us to dislike ourselves even more.
- Try really hard to get other people to like us, and feel horrible when they don't.
- Set goals that bring us little (if any) lasting pleasure.
- Struggle to make decisions.
- Make choices that reflect poor self-insight.
- Lack a sense of purpose in our work.

- Have a distinct feeling that everything we are doing is pointless.

When it is internal, however, we become more interested in:

- Developing our own set of standards to evaluate ourselves.
- Forming our own ideas of how success looks.
- Learning our own innate desires and preferences.
- Figuring out how we feel about other people, rather than obsessing over how they feel about us.
- Setting goals that matter to us.

When a person becomes self-referential, the perception of others becomes secondary. For many of us, this is a really liberating change from the status quo.

Like everyone, I have had my time with struggling against feelings of insecurity. I could paint you a vivid portrait of how I was insecure about my appearance and how I measured myself up against other women throughout my twenties. But the truth is—it isn't all that interesting. It is all of our tales to some degree or another. I don't need to give it any more airtime.

These days, I surprise myself constantly by how unruffled I am (relative to previously) to the shifting tides of other people's moods. And it makes me really happy.

There's something else I have realised about insecurity. When we are self-flagellating and telling ourselves the story that we aren't measuring up, it gives us something to focus on. That is practically comforting compared to the real truth of the situation: that much of life is uncertain. Developing my self-knowledge has helped me to relax into that bigger truth a bit more.

Maybe that seems a little airy-fairy to you. But know that no matter how externally validating you have been until now, that can change and you can become a lot more self-referential. You can become a person who, instead of hiding their irregularities, embraces them.

People will love you for it. But you won't care so much anymore.

Low Self-Esteem

In his song "Say You Won't Let Go," James Arthur croons: "You made me feel like I was enough." I love that song, but this line depresses me a little when I hear it.

We are all affected by feelings of unworthiness, even if we aren't aware of them. Every single one of us is relying on a strategy to alleviate the feeling. The strategy might be helping others or overachieving. We are going to look at what yours could be in Part 4.

I think that when it comes to addressing low self-worth and esteem, it is better not to make it such a focus. I myself have over-focused on this in the past, assuming low self-worth was behind my chain-smoking in my twenties and other compulsive habits.

But low self-worth wasn't the correct diagnosis, I now believe. I behaved compulsively at times because I had trouble with processing certain feelings. When you are hunting for something, you can interpret any behaviour into a 'tell.' We need to be watchful of this.

Self-knowledge can only result in a higher self-esteem because it is what leads us to recognise that we are whole and complete as we are. That sounds so cheesy, I know, but in my experience—it's true.

Not Knowing What We Want

The psychologist Abraham Maslow said: "It isn't normal to know what we want. It is a rare and difficult psychological achievement." Bingo.

Unfortunately, when we don't know what we want, our results in life reflect that. Conversely, those who know what they want tend to get what they want. Napoleon Hill said, "The world has a habit of making room for the man whose words and actions show he knows where he is going." More recently, Ludacris rapped, "Move bitch, get out the way."

It is relatively rare these days to encounter people with real clarity and conviction about the direction they are going across their various life areas. We enjoy a great many options now, which isn't helping (they call it 'the paradox of choice'). And some theorists tell us that some of us (so-called 'maximizers') struggle even more to narrow options, plagued by the desire to choose the best one.

I have real doubts about whether this makes such a big difference. I think that maximizer or not, when we know our innate values, desires and preferences, then having all the choices in the world won't confuse us: we'll be able to easily identify the right thing to do.

If narrowing your options fills you with doubt, you resent making decisions, and frequently go to others to help you to know what you do, you stand to have a whole transformation in this aspect of your life by developing your self-knowledge.

And knowing your values is going to make the biggest difference. We cannot possibly make decent decisions until we know what matters to us. Once we know that, decisions get so much easier because an option is either aligned with our values or it isn't.

In the past, I struggled a lot with knowing what I wanted to do. And I believe the major obstacle was living in my head. When you live in your head, and you are cut off from the wisdom of your feelings, you can wind up making decisions that lack well-roundedness.

And so for me, learning to manage my mind better has improved the position a lot. Now I make big decisions easily. In fact, I enjoy narrowing my options. I feel a lot of resonance with what Greg McKeown says in his book *Essentialism, The Disciplined Pursuit of Less*: "Trade-offs are not something to be ignored or decried. They are something to be embraced and made deliberately, strategically, thoughtfully."

Oh, and I don't really get FOMO('Fear of Missing Out'). FOMO is another symptom of being insecure about our choices.

Feeling a Lack of Purpose

If there was one piece of advice I'd give to my twenty-year-old self it would be to think about purpose a teeny bit more. I'd tell her, "Come on, dude. At least interrupt the thoughts about clothes and makeup with figuring out what lights your fire in life."

Having a sense of purpose in life is constantly identified as being important for human health and happiness. A lack of purpose is thought to be the reason that historically people, and especially men, can fall into a depression after they retire.

Whether legitimate or not, they had been deriving their sense of purpose from earning and bringing home the bacon. (I suspect that in some cases, the emptiness of retirement confronts them with the difficult reality that they never found out who they are and what they actually enjoy doing.)

If we want to avoid the same fate, we need to discover what things bring us purpose. But we needn't make a meal out of it. We start by telling the truth to ourselves and stopping the endless game of distracting ourselves from how we feel.

Chasing Happiness

The writer Thomas Moore says: "Many people think that the point of life is to solve their problems and be happy. But happiness is a fleeting sensation, and you never get rid of problems. Your purpose in life may be to become more of who you are and more engaged with the people and life around you— to really live your life."

Can you relate? I know I did.

Like many people, I used to live like the present moment was an obstacle to overcome to get to the next moment. It made me miserable. Life was progress from want to want rather than from enjoyment to enjoyment.

These days, I feel a lot more awake and content in the moment I am in. This was something I learned once I started paying more attention to what I was doing to undermine my happiness and contentment.

We equate happiness with high-intensity emotions—excitement, anticipation, ecstasy, orgasm. This may be collectively our biggest problem with feeling happier—that we conflate it with pleasure.

But pleasure is not happiness, and high-intensity emotions burn us all out. Ideally what we want is to inhabit what motivational speaker Tony Robbins calls 'a beautiful state.' I'm paraphrasing, but a beautiful state, says Robbins, is when you feel love, joy, gratitude, awe, playfulness, ease, creativity, drive, caring, growth, curiosity and appreciation. This, he says, is how a person looks when they are 'in harmony with essence' (essence being your true nature).

Contrast this with being in a suffering state: stressed out (the overachiever's version of fear), worried, frustrated, angry, depressed, irritable, overwhelmed, resentful and fearful.

Self-knowledge fosters this cooler, but ultimately more sustainable happiness. Even before we have lined life up perfectly, we enjoy the sense that we are making progress. And that feels incredibly satisfying.

3

The Road Ahead

Hopefully I have persuaded you of the benefits of taking a little time to understand that person you call you a little better. I honestly believe that the rewards could be as life-changing for you as they have been for me.

Part 2, which is the most important part of the book, sets out three practices I think of as the reality red pills. These are the practices that have changed my life and that I use each day.

(If you're unfamiliar with the cultural reference, let me help you out: the red pill and its opposite, the blue pill, are popular symbols representing the choice between knowledge, freedom and the sometimes painful truth of reality—red pill—and falsehood, security and the blissful ignorance of illusion—blue pill. In my observations, most of us are on blue pills by default.)

Part 3 sets out the self-knowledge muscles: a list of the personal attributes we need to draw on in the process of knowing ourselves. These personal attributes are worth cultivating in life apart from the pursuit of self-knowledge. They are the same traits that are needed to create happy, fulfilling lives.

Part 4, which looks at the ego-self/self-construct, sets out a key theory that helps explain why you are the way you are. I have found such theories to be essential for growing around my personal weaknesses.

Part 5 is best described with a little analogy: when the artist Michelangelo was asked how he created a piece of sculpture, he answered that the statue already existed within the marble. His job, as he saw it, was to get rid of the excess marble. Part 5 explains how you look once you have gotten rid of your surplus marble.

To wrap up this part, I want to guide you through two reflections that'll help prime you psychologically for the rest of the book.

Be Willing to be Uncomfortable

I was chatting with a friend recently who, upon waking each morning, squeezes a whole lemon and a spoonful of Himalayan salt into a litre of water and chugs it down. When I asked him why he does this, he said he adopted the suggestion instantly after chatting with a dude he met at a party.

This guy was regularly enjoying just about every excess you can think of and swore by the lemon/salt routine for its role in helping him continuing his excesses. In that moment, you could say my friend became emotionally connected with the benefits of the routine. And even stronger, that benefit was represented visually to him.

Before we do anything—and especially things of the non-fun variety—we have to be emotionally connected with the benefits. As author Joe Dispenza says, "The more you learn about the 'what' and the 'why', the easier and more effective the 'how' becomes." (This, by the way, is what I have been trying to do in Part 1. I have been trying to demonstrate the 'why.')

Unless I have been successful in establishing the benefits of working at self-discovery clearly in your mind, or you have already made the links outlined yourself, it'll be difficult for you to adopt any of the suggestions in the rest of this book. More encouragingly on the flip side, if you do want this and do see a benefit, you probably really will succeed in changing your life. Machiavelli said, "Where the willingness is great, the difficulties cannot be great."

Realistically, each new behaviour pattern is hard for a time. The author Mark Manson says: "Everything sucks, some of the time. If you want to be a professional artist, but you aren't willing to see your work rejected hundreds, if not thousands, of times, then you're done before you start. If you want to be a hotshot court lawyer, but can't stand the eighty-hour workweeks, then I've got bad news for you. Because if you love and want something enough—whatever it is—then you don't really mind eating the shit sandwich that comes with it. So what's your favourite flavour of shit sandwich?"

Be willing to eat the occasional shit sandwich. It will serve your self-knowledge and just about everything else.

Know What You Really, *Really* Want

This book is not a self-improvement strategy, it is a guide to self-understanding which removes the feeling like you need to improve. That is an important difference.

When we do work like this, we often think we'll somehow improve. The meditation teacher Pema Chodron—who is probably the most quoted person in this book—describes this tendency as a "subtle aggression against who we really are," and she's right—it is.

It is okay that concerns of self-improvement represent a part of why we make an effort to understand ourselves. We are goal-oriented creatures, and so expecting that to not to matter to us is unrealistic.

But I'd recommend measuring your success by other standards. For example, look at your ability to withstand emotional discomfort, without either catastrophizing or distracting yourself. That is something only you can see and know, but it is a capacity that is hugely impactful on your quality of life.

Ask yourself now what it is that you want to see changes in. And resist being vague about the internal/emotional shifts you desire. The clarity will serve you, plus it is the closest thing you'll get to objective criteria measuring the success of the practices that follow.

It sounds unrealistic to hope to ever lose our attachment to the image of success and happiness. But I have found that that is exactly what happens during self-discovery. You stop being such an 'end-gamer'. Even more amazingly, I appear to be getting the things that I want without being overly controlling about it.

There is this poem by Portia Nelson (it's called "Autobiography in Five Chapters"). It nails how I have found the process of self-discovery—frustratingly slow at times.

She starts by walking into a hole as she walks down the street. On her second walkie, she forgets about the hole and falls into it again. And then she falls a third time, even though she knows it's there, out of pure habit.

Eventually, she walks around the hole.

And finally, she walks down another street.

Part 2

The Reality Red Pills

You take the blue pill, the story ends. You wake up in your bed and believe whatever you want to believe. You take the red pill, you stay in Wonderland, and I show you how deep the rabbit hole goes.

– Morpheus to Neo in The Matrix

The reality red pills—mindfulness, responsibility and acceptance—are not initially things you'd associate with the process of knowing yourself. They seem like spiritual practices that a person does for, say, inner peace.

In truth, you cannot begin to know yourself without them. They are highly practical and absolutely essential.

In addressing the challenges I raised in Part 1, the red pill practices are the most important, foundational things to master. And they are probably already present to varying degrees in your thinking. But so are their opposites:

Truthful state (red pill)	Deception (blue pill)
Mindfulness	Fusion with thoughts and/or feelings
Responsibility	Victim mentality/entitlement/passivity
Acceptance	Denial and escapism

If you want to know yourself, it is essential that your mental state becomes more characteristic of the states of mindfulness, acceptance and responsibility, and less characteristic of reactivity, passivity and non-acceptance.

This part of the book is devoted to looking at how you actually do that.

4

Red Pill #1: Mindfulness

Mindfulness isn't difficult. We just need to remember to do it.

– Sharon Salzburg

Unless you've been living under a rock, you'll already have come across 'mindfulness' several times over. You may even have dabbled in it. I hope so because that'll mean that what follows is repetition rather than anything brand new. And repetition is in the service of learning.

Although mindfulness has only recently been embraced by Western psychology, it is a practice with a long tradition. You can see references to it across various religions, philosophies and spiritual traditions—Buddhism in particular. For Buddhists, mindfulness is an absolute standard. The Buddha himself must be wetting his saffron robes watching us treat mindfulness as though it were the new kale.

So what is mindfulness?

Jon Kabat-Zinn, a world authority on mindfulness, defines it as paying attention in a particular way: on purpose, in the present moment, and non-judgmentally. These are the three elements you need to remember.

- On purpose.
- In the present moment.
- Non-judgmental.

The news anchor and author of the brilliant book *10% Happier*, Dan Harris, describes mindfulness as "the skill of knowing what's happening in your head at any given moment without getting carried away by it."

Practicing mindfulness sounds simple, and it is. But it is not natural for us to pay attention this way. It feels rebellious on the brain initially.

The Opposite of Being Mindful

To understand the important role that mindfulness plays in self-knowledge, it is helpful to briefly consider the opposite way of paying attention. We can do this by flipping Kabat-Zinn's definition around.

When we aren't being purposeful with our attention, we are subject to the undirected mind. Recall from Part 1 that the undirected mind isn't neutral; it has a negativity and fear bias. When we are not being present, we tend to be in our stories and versions of events. And we are definitely the opposite of non-judgmental: we tend to have opinions on every little thing we think, feel and do.

Without mindfulness, there is no separation between the

you that's having the thoughts and sensations, and the you that's aware of that. That means whatever is shouting the loudest gets centre stage (and often what is shouting the loudest isn't something we want to give our attention to).

It isn't too dramatic to say that if we aren't being mindful, we are in a permanent co-dependent relationship with our circumstances, people and the other uncontrollable elements of life. We are highly reactive and succumb easily to whatever our thoughts and emotions tell us to do.

If we receive an irritating text, we are unlikely to be able to stop ourselves from responding reactively. If we have resolved to eat healthier, but we worked through lunch and there is cake in the office, we are unlikely to have a distance enough from our sensation of hunger and stress not to wolf that thing down. We'll ruminate. We'll whip ourselves into anxiety as we spin the world from our seats.

How Mindfulness Addresses Self-Deception

Let's talk a bit more about the ego, which I mentioned in Part 1 but have yet to properly define.

Your ego is the personality and personal reality you created early in life, and whose confines you still operate out of.

It is only through practicing mindfulness that we can hope to develop a sense of our egos as distinct from a state of expansive awareness that we all have. The language of the ego is your thoughts. Mindfulness helps you to realise that you are not your thoughts—you just have them.

As it turns down the language of the thoughts, practicing mindfulness also turns the volume up on our emotions, which communicate with us through the language of our feelings.

From a self-knowledge perspective, understanding and acting on feelings is essential.

The 'stories' we tell ourselves about our experiences are probably the biggest obstacles clouding our judgment. It is the body that is now considered the doorway to the essential nature and that in order to listen carefully to our bodies, we have to drop the storyline and tune into pure sensation. This ability is what a mindfulness practice cultivates.

The Only Other Thing You Need to Know Before You Start

Kabat-Zinn's definition tells us precisely how to practice mindfulness.

There is one further piece of useful information: the distinction between the Thinking and Observing Self. I was first introduced to these terms in Russ Harris' book, *The Happiness Trap: How to Stop Struggling and Start Living*, which I would recommend to anyone that suffers from anxiety or depression.

The Thinking Self is the part of the mind that is responsible for all your thoughts, beliefs, memories, judgments, fantasies. It is the part you identify as 'you'. The Observing Self is the part that is able to be aware of whatever you are thinking or feeling or doing at any moment. It is the record-keeper. Mindfulness is training yourself to operate from the vantage point of the Observing Self.

Many people initially practicing mindfulness choose to use labeling to help them to toggle to the Observing Self. 'Thinking about x now'. 'Feeling anger now'. 'This is called worrying about an illness'. 'This is called being blamed for something I didn't do'. 'This is called disappointment'. You may find labeling useful for driving a wedge between you and your thoughts.

How to Practice Mindfulness

One of the great things about mindfulness is you can do it anytime, anywhere.

If the practice is totally unfamiliar to you, I suggest you formalise a mindfulness practice until you begin to practice automatically. Commit to a certain time of the day, or a certain activity you do each day, spent in a state of mindfulness. Use your commute, for example, to practice paying attention on purpose, in the present moment and non-judgmentally. When you catch your mind wandering or going into a story, bring it back to the three elements.

Let's say I'm practicing mindfulness during a meeting. My attention is with the people in the room and what is being said by the speakers. I am *considering* the information being delivered (TS). I *notice* ('OS') when I slip into daydreaming about what I'll eat for lunch. I am *aware* of irritation and impatience and restlessness, from the way I am breathing (OS).

Or let's take the occasion of a date. My attention is resting on my date and our interactions. I'm focusing on what they're saying and responding to what they're saying (TS). But my attention is divided. I am also *aware* in the background of the thoughts and sensations that are cropping up on the periphery: 'stifling a yawn' or 'self-consciousness ('OS'). The thoughts are like the weather passing through the sky, but I am the sky.

Hopefully you get the gist.

The Difference Between Mindfulness and Meditation

Meditation, which we are getting to later on in the book, is a separate skill to mindfulness. Meditation is the specific process of training your brain to a focus point. For self-knowledge, we need both practices—they are described as a dynamic duo that act to remove the false belief that external factors drive our happiness.

The reason that mindfulness is a reality red pill is that you can do it all the time; it can be a permanent state of being. But being in a permanent state of meditation isn't really possible (or desirable).

That said, meditation is what helps us to practice mindfulness. So we really need to do it, too. More on this later.

5 Things You Might Notice When You Start Practicing Mindfulness

Once you start practicing mindfulness, you should notice a few things you couldn't before:

Opinions and Self-Talk

Learning to observe your opinions is one of the most useful things you can do with your attention.

Internally directed opinions are called self-talk. We all have self-talk, an inner critic with a character which is an amalgamation of various voices, including possibly early critical voices from your childhood. Your mindfulness practice might be the first time you start to become aware of it. Our self-talk gives us a clue about our self-image, or how we see ourselves.

The meditation teacher Sharon Salzberg has given her self-talk a name, Lucy, after a bitchy character from a TV series. She greets Lucy during her mindfulness practice and sometimes even tells her to chill out. This gentle mocking is the perfect response to the nasty inner critic. When we become aware of negative self-talk, gradually, we can begin to abandon it. That's a self-love strategy.

As for your opinions about other people and the world, I'll just go ahead and say it: a lot of them are worthless. (Hey, it's just an opinion—take it or leave it.)

To me, at this stage, the most useful/interesting thing about my opinions is what they tell me first about my physiological state, and second, about my Hidden Self, which we are going to look at in Part 4. Most of my opinions serve no additional value than that. And often, they are precisely what prevent me from behaving in generous ways towards others, when I'm not actively aware of them.

I haven't had fewer opinions since I started practicing mindfulness: in fact, I am even more keenly aware of them. However, I don't pay so much attention to them. And that, my friends, feels like freedom and progress.

In his book *The Untethered Soul*, Michael Singer says, "You are capable of ceasing the absurdity of listening to the perpetual problems of your psyche. You can put it to an end." Thank goodness, this has proven to be true in my own life.

Your 'Attachments'

Practicing mindfulness helps you to become aware of how attachments pull and push you during your day and life. Attachments are a concept I found through Buddhist teachings. Buddhism philosophy basically says that attachments are the root cause of all suffering we experience.

When you feel an attachment, it just means you feel a sort

of clinging or a recoiling. The clinging kind is an attraction or desire. The recoiling kind is an aversion.

We all have different desires and aversions, although many of us share the same ones, too.

The point of becoming aware of attachments is that (eventually, hopefully) it might help to create a state of detachment, which is close to an ideal state.

Detachment, the opposite state of attachment, is being present whilst carrying the awareness that everything is temporary, albeit some things do last longer than others. It liberates us from the suffering that clinging or running creates.

When you are in a state of attachment, it is difficult to realise your potential. For example, working towards your highest aspirations always has a confronting element, whereby aversions to pain and discomfort, and addiction to pleasure and safety, are push/pulling us away from what matters.

Practicing mindfulness is the largest step you can take in loosening the grip your attachments have over you because it is through mindfulness that we become aware that 'I am attached right now' or 'I am averted right now.' This is the start. From there, awareness then opens up the possibility of acting in spite of our attachments.

Your Defences

Psychological defence mechanisms are unconscious strategies or mind tricks we use to keep our version of reality intact. Practicing mindfulness is how we become aware of using defence mechanisms, which is key to eventually disarming them.

In his brilliant book, *Why do I do that?*, Joseph Burgo

explained that we use the defence mechanisms to defend for three areas of psychological concern:

- Bearing need and dependency as an inevitable part of relationships.
- Managing intense emotions.
- Developing a sense of self-esteem.

Here is a list of the defence mechanisms:

- Repression and denial.
- Displacement and reaction formation.
- Splitting.
- Idealisation.
- Projection.
- Control.
- Thinking.
- Narcissism, blaming and contempt (all defences against shame).

These are a whole new language to learn (and on that front, I really recommend reading Burgo's book). But once you know them, you can recognise them in yourself. Again, that isn't really possible without practicing mindfulness.

Your Hidden Beliefs

Practicing mindfulness clues us into our beliefs that aren't always within easy grasp of awareness.

Please note that I did not say limiting beliefs. Honestly, if that phrase would disappear from the face of the earth, I wouldn't miss it.

The reason I don't like this phrase is I just think people get too fixated on the idea of having limited beliefs to overcome. The idea that our limiting beliefs are what cause us to self-sabotage is promulgated in personal growth circles. According to the prevailing view, if you keep messing up or not making good on your plans, you probably have a limiting belief preventing you from taking life by the balls in whatever the life area.

Belief in a limiting belief can itself be a limiting belief. I prefer these days to practice mindfulness and use the insights to tell me where I could be potentially holding unhelpful beliefs.

The Many Ways You Move Your Cheese

A reference to the popular book, *Who Moved My Cheese?*, this is about how mindfulness clues us into our own forms of negativity. Everyone has a thing or things that they do—'sad songs,' if you like. Mindfulness allows you notice them.

The motivational teacher Tony Robbins says that energy-sapping lines of thinking fall into one of three categories: lost, less, or never variety. We might be buying into the story that we lost something, we have less of something, or we will never have something.

I think that for me, it's less. In the past, I would make things I had not enough somehow, which caused me to disappear large chunks of time into planning possibilities for the future.

Your mindfulness practice will help you to notice your own stories.

How Without Mindfulness, Your Future is Fixed

Here is a terrifying idea that should really inspire you to practice mindfulness if the above didn't do it.

Without mindfulness, we are only capable of perceiving life through the lens of past experiences. That's because you never separate yourself from your thoughts, and your thinking is a product of what you already know. And so we can say that if you aren't practicing mindfulness every day, you're heading for a very specific and predictable destiny.

In his book *You are the Placebo*, Joe Dispenza says: "Thinking the same thoughts leads us to make the same choices. Making the same choices leads to demonstrating the same behaviours. Demonstrating the same behaviours leads us to create the same experiences. Creating the same experiences leads us to produce the same emotions. And those same emotions then drive the same thoughts."

I don't know about you, but I don't necessarily want my past to shape my future.

Mindfulness is the only option.

Summary

So that's our first reality red pill: mindfulness. Hopefully we are in agreement on how essential is it to self-knowledge. What are you waiting for? Start practicing right away.

The ultimate goal of mindfulness is to move us away from interpreting reality as part of our ongoing narratives, and instead see reality as it is. In Buddhism, this is called *prajna* (meaning 'direct insight').

Now let's look at the other two reality red pill practices.

5

Red Pill #2: Responsibility

It's not the events of our lives that shape us, but our beliefs as to what these events mean.

– *Tony Robbins*

Responsibility was a teaching that brutally slapped me on the face aged 29. I'll tell you about that at the end of this section. For now, let's just say that responsibility was a revelation to me and continues to support my self-knowledge, freedom and happiness.

Taking responsibility means exercising your power to select the meaning you attribute to the events of your life, as well as your ability to take action. The practice reflects the truth that our perspectives and our actions are the only things we have genuine control over. Therefore, it makes sense to put energy mostly into those things.

The first message—that we control our perspective—is one

that has come at us time and time again. Stories from *Alice in Wonderland* to *The Matrix* have hinted at the ultimate state of things: that there is no objective reality. We make the meaning as we go along.

The idea is also supported by quantum physics, which now tells us we collapse our attention around certain points, and that this is the basis for the reality we experience. In other words: we see what we want to see.

Weirdly, almost nobody behaves like this is true. Here is what we generally do instead:

- Choose the least empowering perspective available.
- Lie to ourselves about not having a choice in our circumstances.
- Focus on how our current situation is limiting us rather than figuring out what we can do from where we are.
- Waste time and energy on things we don't have control over.

Here is what we do with our capacity to take action:

- Wait for things to come to us—also known as entitlement.
- Hope that other people will 'help' or 'save' us and maybe even orchestrate it so they do—also known as playing the victim.

These attitudes get us off the hook from taking action necessary to change our situations. Taking responsibility is initially the harder option. But ultimately life is happier when you do.

To illustrate and to lighten things up around here, I will tell you a story of a romantic mishap from my recent past.

What Happened in Detroit

First, a little context: prior to my brain burp with responsibility, I wasn't choosing perspectives that empowered me. I succumbed to whatever interpretations my thoughts and emotions came up with. I also wasted my attention on things I couldn't control (other people's opinions). I justified staying in negative jobs and unhealthy relationships on the pretense that I had to. There were basically leaks in all buckets.

I've been using this teaching a lot in the past five years to gradually take back control of my life. Among its most awesome effects is how much more empowered I feel in my love life. My close friends will tell you I am now relatively fearless in love. This teaching is why.

On to the story:

If you were paying really close attention, you will recall from the introduction that I mentioned taking a detour to Detroit from New York on my route back to London. Well, I was going to spend time with a guy who lived there and who I had met when he was on a bachelor weekend in Playa Del Carmen.

We had spent approximately two highly intoxicated hours in each other's company that evening but had stayed in touch sporadically between when we met and when I rocked up to Detroit five months later. I know, pretty crazy and adventurous.

Overall, it was an interesting experience, but it did end in disappointment for me. The guy had never really entertained the idea of something long term with me. I had misjudged that he was as open to that as I was, and I felt like a bit of an idiot about it.

What I realised was that there were clear signs that he wasn't treating me as a serious prospect and I had been ignoring them. I wanted that trip to Detroit to happen so much, that I had created this whole fantasy of a relationship in my head which bore very little semblance to reality.

Blaming ourselves for silly mistakes can just be another distraction from taking responsibility—another form of misapplied control. I don't tend to play the blame game so much these days. Instead, I let myself feel my hurt feelings (another relative novelty to me), before allowing that experience to instruct me going forward.

And you know what? Romantic and other disappointments are never quite the same after you apply the responsibility teaching. When you've taken control over your ability to attribute meaning, you drop endlessly spinning on painful interpretations.

You take what you need to know—and then you move the fuck on with your life.

Owning Your Half

If I ever get a tattoo, I will have this one placed on my butt cheeks so I can expose myself to my mates whenever we are analysing the latest failed romance:

"Yes, yes—but what really happened?"

It never fails to amaze me how vague everyone is about what went wrong when an unfavourable romantic outcome happens. Or how unwilling we are to make a genuine attempt to understand how two people's expectations have gotten so out of whack. And also how quick we are to write things off as being due to the other person being 'crazy' or 'mental' or whatever. (I am particularly bored of that one.)

People disappoint and hurt us all the time. But often, if we are willing to look closely enough, we can see that we generated expectations on the other person that aren't based on the real world position. Or else we ignored things because it suited us to do so. And that happens when we are in need in some way. It can happen so easily when we don't feel whole and complete on our own.

As the deciders of our dispositions, we have the ability to judge, evaluate, endorse, reject or accept whatever we choose. So even if options are unexpectedly removed from us—like happy-ever-afters with sexy American dudes—we still get to choose how we feel about that. That is where the power of the human spirit lies. We choose even if we lose.

This applies to our work, too. A lot of us are in the precise struggle of having spent years and cash investing in a career that we find doesn't suit us at all. And our dissatisfaction is the fuel for a great many low-level addictions, as well as an inflated importance of weekend and holiday time. (Strictly speaking, it is running from our dissatisfaction fueling those things. If dissatisfaction were simply allowed to do its job, we'd never get into such a mess.)

When we acknowledge our responsibility, we finally own the truth that it is within our power to change our circumstances and take the steps to get ourselves out of the hole. For jobs we feel stuck in, that might be finding new possibilities to be engaged in the work we are being paid well to do. Or yes—actually leaving!

Only you know whether you are using alluring self-justifications to stay a powerless victim of your life and circumstances. You won't get any judgment from me. I have done that myself for years. I've stayed in a relationship and a job past their due dates. That's how I know how soul-destroying it is.

If this speaks to your situation right now, I would like to make one suggestion: that you at least tell the truth to yourself.

Even when we aren't ready to make a change, it is always more empowering to admit: "I am choosing to stay or leave, even though nothing is compelling me—my hands aren't tied here. Perhaps I don't know why I am making these choices yet, but I have to assume there is a payoff somewhere because I continue to make them."

There is a funny thing about truth. Eventually, it's what sets a person free.

The Things We Can't Control

It is possible to take the responsibility teaching too far. (In actuality, it isn't the teaching but a distorted application of it that I am going to talk to you about now).

Some things are not in our control. The quality of our parenting is a good one.

There are such things as happenstance, fortune and luck. When we deny the existence of those things, it isn't self-compassionate.

I used to take responsibility too far, seeing everything about my life as an extension or reflection of who I was being. I felt powerful, yes, but there was no tonality there. It is also incredibly egotistical to see things this way.

The Austrian psychiatrist Viktor Frankl was placed in a Nazi concentration camp. That's something he couldn't control.

Challenged by some objectively awful circumstances, Frankl described how he was called upon to take responsibility for his experience of the camp. Ultimately, he finds a sense of purpose during his time there: helping others to find their purpose. This choice is 'the last vestiges are freedom.' In his epic book, *Man's Search for Meaning*, he said:

> *When we are no longer able to change a situation, we are challenged to change ourselves. Everything can be taken from a man but one thing: the last of the human freedoms—to choose one's attitude in any given set of circumstances, to choose one's own way.*

This quote—Frankl's whole life—is a great testament to the power of responsibility. He made lemonade from the bitterest lemons out there.

The Law of Attraction

The Law of Attraction has become decent bait for heavily rational people to mock the spiritually inclined. A believer in the Law of Attraction believes that our reality reflects our level of thought. This may remind you of responsibility as defined here. But they are not quite the same.

I like the Law of Attraction, because it has made people become aware of their thoughts. But if whenever something good happens, we say we 'manifested' it, we are setting ourselves up for some blowback when reality bites.

It is a lot saner to take the view that 'whatever is happening,

I'll not struggle against it'. This way we stand the best chance of not throwing in the towel on managing our attention.

I recently learned of an upgrade to the Law of Attraction: the 'loving what arises' teaching (it is from Matt Khan who wrote *Whatever Arises, Love That*, if you're interested). In loving what arises, no matter what happens, you see it as a learning opportunity. You don't value the good over the bad. You employ the idea that whatever is happening is useful for helping you to awaken to the next level of integrity in yourself. It has been revelatory for me to apply this mindset to life. Pema Chodron said, "The very moment is the perfect teacher." She is speaking of the same thing.

We are creating our own reality all the time. But it doesn't happen through manifesting girlfriends and boyfriends and cars. Rather, it happens through the humble work of managing our internal experience. It is about expressing and experiencing things.

The other problematic application of the Law of Attraction teaching is people can believe that thinking alone is enough. But as we all know really, positive thinking needs to be combined with action. In other words, to attain what we seek, we must believe we deserve it and our actions need to reflect that.

How to Practice Responsibility

As with mindfulness, practicing responsibility is not hard. It is just a perspective that you adopt. Over time, it can become your default way of looking at things.

Begin by asking yourself honestly whether there is any entitlement, victim mentality, or self-justifications in your thinking (and we will look at how to recognise those things now), and whether you are wasting energy on things you can't control.

You can then use our mindfulness practice to suss out how you are not taking responsibility in your life and slowly begin to take the reins on that.

Enemies of Responsibility: Self-Entitled Thinking

Let's now aim to improve our awareness of the enemies of responsibility.

One of those is entitlement. Entitlement is characterised by the quality of 'I deserve' or 'I don't want this. I want it my way.' It is having unjustified expectations on others and life.

Entitlement stands in the way of responsibility because it puts us in the passive position of waiting for/expecting things to come to us.

Entitlement is fairly common. Author, motivational speaker and marketing consultant, Simon Sinek, says it's a characteristic of Millennials due to failed parenting strategies. In his book *The Power of Myth*, Joseph Campbell says it's sort of inherent in the process of development:

"We are in a condition of dependency under someone's protection and supervision for some fourteen to twenty-one years—and if you are going on for your Ph.D, this may continue to perhaps thirty-five. You are in no way a self-responsible, free agent but an obedient dependent, expecting and receiving punishments and rewards. To evolve out of this position of psychological immaturity to the courage of self-responsibility and assurance requires a death and a resurrection."

Not all expectations are unjustified. I personally have expectations for my friends that they will treat my time with the same respect that they treat theirs (for example). In psyche speak, this is called 'having boundaries,' which is necessary. The author Iylana Vanzant says, "Boundaries create a structure and parameter for what is and is not accepted, permitted, accommodated, and tolerated in your presence and space."

You probably know deep down when your expectations are unjustified. For example, being entitled at work may look like expecting to enjoy all elements of it, and to fulfill you without you making an effort to organise your job so that it is fulfilling. We never try to make things better for ourselves when we are entitled. To steal a term from Robert Greene, it results in a lot of 'dead time' when we blame other people or circumstances for our misfortunes.

Entitlement makes you less successful too. In his book *The Slight Edge: Turning Simple Disciplines into Massive Success,* Jeff Olsen says: "The predominant state of mind displayed by those people on the failure curve is blame. The predominant state of mind displayed by those people on the success curve is responsibility."

When we take responsibility for our frustrations, we are immediately a lot more empowered to act. That is the correct use of the state of dissatisfaction.

The Other Enemy: Victim Mentality

I don't think any of us consciously choose victim mentality; it just becomes a habit. Being a victim is characterised by the desire for others to help us and feel bad for us. As a pattern of behaviour, it must feel hugely disempowering.

An extreme version of victim mindset is learned helplessness: the pervasive feeling that what you do will not, or cannot, make a difference. People develop learned helplessness due to an experience early in life; it's a proven 'inability' to make things better. We all get defeated by ourselves, but a person affected by learned helplessness made the defeat wholesale (something that pessimists tend to do).

Both conditions can be reversed by practicing taking responsibility. When we finally see ourselves as in control of our lives, the idea of anyone else having to deliver something loses appeal.

Now I want to mention something I did in my late twenties that helped me to live responsibility and that you may also be interested in.

Girl, Interrupted: Responsibility Immersion Training

When I was 29, I found myself sitting in a room with 150 or so others while an Australian guy named David was yelling at us that everything we knew was wrong. It was Friday morning. This went on until late into the hours on Sunday.

Some of you will instantly recognise the format of the Landmark Forum—the legendary training seminar based on the principles developed by American critical thinker and author Werner Erhard. The seminar 'promises to transform your ability to experience living,' and it does (it did for me). Similar to Gestalt therapy, the emphasis is on personal responsibility.

Doing Landmark was really game-changing for me. I won't go into that too much here and now. I wrote a more in-depth account of my experience at Landmark here [artofwellbeing.com/2017/06/21/landmark-forum/] I just wanted to mention it as an option to consider.

My view is that if you have the spare cash, then doing Landmark or a comparable immersion programme (Google it—there are a few out there) is a great investment in your growth. It is not necessary, but it can help to lodge these teachings into your brain quite quickly. People find such things more transformational than reading a book because of the experiential element.

Summary

Our internal reactions to the events of life are entirely under our control. There lies our power and our freedom to create our own reality. Without using that power, we are like chess pawns being played by life and other people.

Responsibility is also the only thing that makes the uncertainty of life manageable. In this way, it is deeply courage-building.

6

Red Pill #3: Acceptance

Life creates situations that push you to your edges, all with the effect of removing what is blocked inside of you. In order to grow, you must give up the struggle to remain the same and learn to embrace change at all times.

– Michael Singer

Acceptance is the third and final reality red pill and probably the most difficult one to swallow. In a self-knowledge context, acceptance means being attentive to your full emotional spectrum, most importantly, negative emotions. It is personal growth gold.

Whereas mindfulness fosters a kind of choiceless awareness, acceptance is noticing where you are struggling against certain emotions and deliberately dropping that struggle. This, of course, is the last thing we tend to want to do. It feels like the metaphorical equivalent of pressing the bruise.

Implicit in the acceptance teaching is the idea of using external events of life as material to 'work on' rather than events to avoid. When we commit to acceptance, we do not try to escape from present circumstances for a long period or even a short period. Escaping unpleasantness dulls our capacity to feel positive emotions over time which may explain why we need to manufacture pleasure as we do, with alcohol and other stimulants.

We deny our emotions for good reasons. We are scared of what it means to feel all the sadness and loneliness that we do. Existing within a culture that has a happiness bias doesn't help.

However, as any decent therapist would tell you, a more legitimate concern is the damage done to the psyche by unprocessed emotions. If you ignore feelings for long enough, that will have some sort of a limiting consequence in your life.

When we accept things, we stop fearing your own thoughts quite so much. After a period, we feel a lot more resilient.

Weirdly, it is only through accepting all of our emotions that our regular emotions begin to change. Describing the well-known Acceptance Paradox, Carl Rogers said, "The curious paradox is that when I accept myself just as I am, then I can change."

Our Environment of Non-Acceptance

In the West, we tend to treat emotions like speed bumps that slow us down in reaching our goals. We generally do not practice acceptance.

What doesn't help is that now, thanks to technology, the fiction of other people's success/abundance/happiness is in our faces, making the opposite states feel even more unnatural and alien. It is also easier to escape and distract ourselves. This means our resolve for facing up to things is weaker and weaker.

It isn't just technology that makes acceptance harder. You probably have a lineage of non-acceptance, just as I do. Humans balk at unpleasant, uncomfortable things. And we repress each other by not accepting aspects of human nature. For example, men are generally discouraged from demonstrating emotion. Women might be discouraged from expressing their power and strength.

Without Acceptance, We Don't Use Our Emotions Correctly

Non-acceptance basically cuts us off from the instructive potential of our emotions. Instead, it keeps us distracted by the secondary problems that our underlying emotions create.

One apparent/surface-level problem might be that we cannot lose weight. The issue may stem from using food to avoid uncomfortable feelings or great sadness. Over time, we can't even see what we are doing. We just assume we are greedy or whatever.

Feelings, called the language of the heart, offer us much guidance—as much, if not more, than our thoughts. By being selective about the emotions we permit, we stay ignorant of internal guidance.

How Do I Know What I Am Not Accepting?

If you're human, then it is safe to assume that you avoid certain feelings. Avoiding pain is a human impulse. In Freudian psychoanalysis, this impulse is called 'the pleasure principle.' In

Buddhism, pleasure-seeking is referred to as 'samsara' which is the instinctual seeking of pleasure and avoiding of pain in order to satisfy biological and psychological needs. The pleasure principle is so powerful that it is even responsible for shaping our identities, which we are going to look at in Part 4.

So how do you know what you aren't accepting?

Repressing anything takes a constant psychological effort, and what gives the game away usually is the presence of a compulsive habit, addiction or dependency. When you start practicing acceptance, you may find that compulsiveness or addictive behaviour patterns drop away (this is what has happened in my own life). Many bad habits stem from escaping the moment we meet our emotional edge and we just can't stand it. We become addicted to whatever pads the pain.

My Story of Non-Accepting

I was in my thirties when my lifelong habit of avoiding difficult emotions came to the fore.

Around the time my parents got divorced when I was 11, I gained a lot of weight quickly. I didn't know it at the time, of course, but I was dealing with the extreme sadness I felt by using food/comfort eating. Although I eventually lost the weight by the time I was 16, the pattern of using substances to deal with my emotions was set. Through my twenties, I branched out to weed and alcohol. It was always things with me, rather than people because I never felt I could rely on other people to get what I needed (which is a whole other issue I have needed to deal with).

When I learned that compulsive behaviour was a clue pointing towards unacknowledged feelings, it made sense. I began to become curious about exactly how I felt right before I binged on food or numbed myself with weed, or felt the desire to get excessively drunk on alcohol. What was I feeling?

Like me, what you'll likely find is that if you've denied a certain emotion in yourself for long enough, you'll actually stop realizing when you're feeling it. This is what had happened.

I have slowly weaned myself off using substances to meet my needs, and now I aim to give whatever I am feeling permission instead. And guess what? Letting myself feel was never as overwhelming as I had imagined. It was a lot easier than dealing with the emotional baggage of repeatedly overeating or smoking.

When you feel out of control with something, it affects you. You feel like you don't trust yourself and you can't just relax. It can really undermine your self-confidence.

Since practicing acceptance, I do not control, I'm not excessive, and I am relaxed. This has been a big improvement in my quality of life.

I am not saying that when we practice acceptance, that is all we need to do in order to take control over our addictions. It really depends on how ingrained the behaviour pattern is, among other things. But the stuff we get addicted to—junk food, alcohol, drugs—become a lot less compelling when we aren't so dedicated to escaping unpleasant, uncomfortable feelings.

How to Practice Acceptance

Like the other two reality red pills, it is simple to accept. It takes a values shift to begin with. For inspiration and guidance, let's hear from Pema Chodron again:

Generally speaking, we regard discomfort in any form as bad news. But for...people who have a certain hunger to know what is true—feelings like disappointment, embarrassment, irritation, resentment, anger, jealousy and fear, instead of being bad news, are actually very clear moments that teach us where we are holding back.

We basically need to be like those people with hunger. The practice kicks in upon the first moment of awareness of something in your experience:

1. Our mindfulness practice leads us to notice we have the unpleasant thought, emotion or sensation.
2. We experience the urge to escape it somehow but we don't.
3. Instead, we try waiting a while and asking, "What am I feeling?" Allow whatever needs to come up to come up.
4. Watch any thoughts or analysis that bubble up and pass by. Keep the focus on knowing the feeling instead.

Chodron says:

Rather than letting our negativity get the better of us, we could acknowledge that right now we feel like a piece of shit and not be squeamish about taking a good look. That's the compassionate thing to do. That's the brave thing to do.

We could smell the piece of shit. We could feel it; what is its texture, colour and shape?

We can explore the nature of that piece of shit. We can know the nature of dislike, shame and embarrassment and not believe there is something wrong with that. We can drop the fundamental hope that there is a better 'me' who will one day emerge. We can't just jump over ourselves as if we were not there. It's better to take a straight look at all our hopes and fears.

There are several mindfulness-based techniques you can use to help you to practice acceptance. If you feel like non-acceptance is a big issue for you, I really recommend reading Tara Brach's book, *Radical Acceptance*.

Acceptance Has Wider Benefits, Too

When we practice acceptance, we become a lot more compassionate. That is because it is only to the degree that we embrace ourselves and all of our ugly messy parts that we can do the same for others.

The more that we integrate, the more we begin to see others beyond their own divided, unconscious states. The qualities of patience, acceptance, forgiveness and compassion become cornerstones of our encounters—no matter who we are dealing with!

Summary

The practice of acceptance has been described as 'a subtle form of annihilation' and 'the cornerstone of an awakened consciousness.' Having been practicing for a while, I can see why. Often, the things we are called upon to accept are the very things we have previously worked hard to exclude from our awareness. It can feel very unsettling to let that stuff in.

But acceptance, which equates to treating yourself as valid and whole, is how you become more of who you really are. Put another way, practicing acceptance is how you become truly authentic and authenticity is freedom.

If acceptance were lyrics of a song, they'd be these ones from Leonard Cohen:

Ring the bells that can still ring.
Forget your perfect offering.
There is a crack, a crack in everything.
That's how the light gets in.

Part 3

The Self-Knowledge Muscles

Many of us labour under the delusion that we're permanently stuck with all of the difficult parts of our personalities—that we're 'hot-tempered', or 'shy', or 'sad'—and that these are fixed, immutable traits.

We now know that many of the attributes we value most are, in fact, skills, which can be trained the same way you build your body in the gym.

This is radical, hopeful stuff.

– Dan Harris

If the red pills are like a pair of truth-telling sunglasses, these muscles are the necessary items in your beach kit. They're in a symbiotic relationship. The muscles help you to practice the red pills—and the sunglasses help you to find the things in your bag.

Here they are:

- Into the woods—the skill of being alone/reflecting.
- Just say no—the skill of saying no.
- IDK—the skill of having humility and managing uncertainty.
- Roy Walker—the skill of being able to recognise and name your emotions.
- #Nofilter—the skills of listening and speaking without ego.
- Letting go—the skill of detachment.
- Eye of the Tiger—the skill of having courage.
- Christian Grey—the skill of mastering your mind.

Reading these, they may occur to you as personal attributes rather than skills:

1. Introspective and reflective.
2. Wise and discerning.
3. Humble.
4. Emotionally intelligent.
5. Good communicator.
6. Spiritually evolved.
7. Brave.
8. Self-disciplined.

To that I would say—you're right!

The reason I have chosen to present them as skills over traits is because of something I like to call 'the dogmatic I am': the phenomenon of treating our personalities as something fixed. Like somehow, if we haven't been something yet (or if we think we haven't), that means we never can.

This is a problem. Self-concepts have an annoying habit of being self-fulfilling. As the writer Gary Szenderski says: "'I am' triggers thoughts, actions and events that will confirm what we believe. We literally live up to our own declarations of self."

Psychologists are now saying that our personalities are memorised states. We have the choice at any time to discard behaviours that aren't serving us. This is the possibility that awareness opens up.

I used to view myself as a scatterbrained serial procrastinator with no capacity for follow-through. It wasn't a conscious line of thought, but it was evident from the way I failed to fully commit to things that this was how I saw myself. And I really have embodied those traits for a large percentage of my life.

Until I learned that I was not those things, it was simply self-reinforcing. It was only because I had shaken that belief that I was able to start working on this book. It took over two years of keeping a blog and not quitting to prove to my brain that I could stick to a writing commitment of this magnitude.

It sounds ridiculous to defend such an unhelpful self-concept. But that is what we do. I think it is born out of that craving for certainty that we all have.

Humans are highly adaptive which we tend to forget.

If nothing else, this part of the book should be a reminder of that truth.

7

The Into the Woods Muscle

*I went to the woods because I wished to live deliberately,
to front only the essential facts of life, and see if I could not
learn what it had to teach, and not, when I came to die,
discover that I had not lived.*

– *Henry David Thoreau*

This muscle is about being okay with being alone. Spending time alone is necessary to develop self-knowledge and important for other things, too, such as healthy relationships. If you know that you avoid solitude right now, then I'm excited for how magical your life is going to be when you no longer do.

It doesn't matter how introverted or extroverted you are. I don't care; it's irrelevant. Introverts and extroverts both need time by themselves. And from my observations, introverted people are not necessarily more self-aware then extroverted people because they tend to stake out alone time. It is what you do with the time that matters.

Why is Alone Time So Necessary for Deeper Self-Knowledge?

There are several reasons.

A big one is when you're spending all of your time with others, it's easy to forget what's important to you. It isn't just that we are influenced by the opinions/actions of others. It is more that we naturally want to harmonise and fit in, or to dominate. Either way, some kind of relational concern is apparent. It is distracting.

Another reason is our tendency to prioritise the needs of others over our own. During solitude is where we can reflect at length on topics of concern.

In summary, compromises happen of all kinds. Jean de la Bruyere said, "All men's misfortunes spring from their hatred of being alone." This may not be overstating things.

Other people are not always the enemy of self-knowledge; our interactions with others can help us to know ourselves. We are going to return to that topic later.

Why We Resist Solitude

Being alone is such a simple thing, but many of us struggle to do it. It can force us to confront things about ourselves that are incongruent with our self-image: thoughts like we aren't all that happy and we don't really like ourselves, for example. Pink sang, "The quiet scares me 'cause it screams the truth." Yep.

We're also afraid of silence because we equate it with insignificance. This was a big thing for me. It is natural to want to be heard and seen. It has taken me a long time to stop going to my smartphone for validation and a sense that I am important in this world. And it is still a bit of a nervous tic I have, although it has shrunk significantly.

If you do feel uncomfortable with the idea of solitude, or find that you use alone time unwisely, try to figure out what is underneath that. Figure out what it is you are telling yourself about alone time.

Here are two common perceptions that make solitude off-putting:

'I'll Feel Lonely'

Solitude does not equate to your feeling lonely. Feeling lonely is where you're alone and wanting company. But a person can be alone for chunks of time without ever desiring company.

Sometimes we will feel lonely. This is a fact of life. This happens even when we aren't alone; I have experienced loneliness with other people at times.

We all need to learn not to fear loneliness. It affects our self-discovery efforts because it likely means we will go out of our way to engage in pursuits that have no meaning for us. And doing that will keep us from enjoying a life that is hugely meaningful.

The blogger Leo Babauta says:

We will socialize endlessly, including on social networks and email. To avoid being alone, we'll end up with someone who isn't really good for us, just to have someone to cling to, someone to rely on. We'll eat junk food or shop to comfort ourselves, because these things are replacements for love.

Practicing mindfulness and acceptance helps us to bring our attention to lonely feelings and stay with them without grabbing for entertainment. Another thing you can try is shifting how you view loneliness. It is a sort of cognitive reframing exercise that I have found useful in the past.

In her book *When Things Fall Apart,* Pema Chodron identifies six qualities of 'cool' (as in non-urgent feeling) loneliness. They are almost like benefits really:

- Less desire.
- Contentment.
- Avoiding unnecessary activity.
- Complete discipline.
- Not being so confronted by tempting things/ opportunities.
- Not hiding from difficult thoughts.

They are lines of thinking that help you to form a new appreciation for loneliness. In my most recent spell of 'cool' loneliness, I found great comfort from these.

I have also found that acknowledging that you are feeling lonely does not stop you from enjoying being where you are or doing what you are doing. As with accepting anything, allowing yourself to feel lonely at times makes a more complex reality available: that you can be lonely and happy at the same time. This improves what's called your emotional diversity—your ability to feel a wide range of feelings.

Feeling lonely can also be useful information. For me, it helped me to see that my values had adjusted slightly so that I needed to spend more time with my family and friends over travelling. Feeling that feeling affected the decisions I made subsequently.

'It's Boring'

If it isn't fear of loneliness keeping solitude at bay, then it's our terminal fear of being bored. Solitude plus minimal distractions can seem extremely under-stimulating for a breed of smartphone addicts.

Practicing mindfulness might lead you to the conclusion that boredom is an illusion of the mind—a story about how we should be spending the time.

As with loneliness, we can also reframe moments of boredom as the potential to develop a dying skill: creative thought. I bet that like me, as soon as there is an opening in life, you plug that gap with your smartphone. This encourages a dependent state of mind where we go to the outside world for solutions.

The writer David Foster Wallace said, "If you are immune to boredom, there is literally nothing you cannot accomplish." He must have been referring to the possibilities for creative thought that can open up when a person lets themselves get a little bored every now and then.

I really recommend letting yourself feel bored every now and then. Resist the lure of checking your phone on every single train journey, etc.

It is said that when we truly engage with the world and focus on our goals, we're never bored. In my experience, that is true.

How I Came to Embrace Solitary Time

My own transformation with using bouts of solitude to deepen my self-knowledge has happened slowly.

At this point in my life, I probably live a more contemplative style than most would feel comfortable with or is even possible. My work and my daily activities are of the basically solitary variety. And in addition, because of writing this book, I have been taking periods where I scale down everything possible in life to dedicate myself to it. I'm an extrovert living the life of an introvert!

Did I ever think I would be the type of person that took writing sabbaticals? No. I prefer the company of others (and especially people I find interesting), but I do not prevent this from doing what I want to do. And in order to get this book finished alongside my working commitments, really, this was the only option.

It is my belief and my experience that solitude helps us to be with others in a more conscious and aware way. I see my alone periods as improvers of my ability to be with others. Aside from making me appreciate people more, I feel like I am more present with them, having been so present with myself.

If you feel like you need additional support with this to begin with, there are environments that support quiet time for reflection. In fact, it was through the practice of fasting (which like solitude, is a cessation on consumption) that I was awoken to the profound clarity I'd have after a short period of minimal company and chatter.

It can take time, so be patient. In his book *Soul Friends*, Steven Cope suggests that our ability to be alone is contingent on having an early experience of being safe in the presence of another. I don't know what your upbringing was like, but be aware that that is a potential issue for you, and be patient with yourself as you get better at being alone.

The Art of Reflection

Reflection is one of the main activities we do in solitary time. It is an extremely important activity for us to do, and not just for self-knowledge. Studies have found that those who were prompted to use their commute to think about and plan for the day were happier, more productive and less burned out.

There are common misuses of our reflective capacities: ruminating on the past and overthinking about the future for example. These things are counterproductive to self-knowledge because they result in reality distortions.

How to Stop Ruminating

If you know you're a ruminator, then stopping yourself may seem like a lofty aim. But it can happen. I believe it can be done through practicing mindfulness along with meditation, which we are going to look at soon.

How do you know when you're ruminating as distinct from healthily reflecting? Tune in to how you feel. If reflection is freaking you out, then you are ruminating. Remember that rumination rehearses—there is usually an element of interpreting and reinterpreting your emotional state.

When reflecting on something that has happened, the focus should be 'what', i.e. 'what am I feeling?' rather than 'why do I feel this bad?'

The other big tell that you are ruminating is that you are

doing a lot of thinking and not much action. Ruminating prevents us taking action which is what people suffering from depression tend to do. When a person is depressed, there is the tendency for them to ruminate about how their depression interferes with their life.

Avoiding Overthinking

I'm not much of a ruminator, but overthinking I can do! Overthinking, or 'feasting on our own thoughts' (Plato), is another very common plague and misuse of our reflective capacities.

If you're like me and you have spent a lot of your life overthinking, then this is one of your biggest obstacles to self-knowledge and (believe it or not) also good judgment. Alan Watts said, "A person who thinks all the time has nothing to think about except thoughts, so he loses touch with reality and lives in a world of illusions." A world of illusions—sounds about right.

Overthinking, planning or obsessing can give us a false sense of productivity. I am convinced that it is another reaction to the uncertainty of life. I believe that overthinking, like insecurity, is just another of our doomed attempts at control.

That is why mindfulness and responsibility are the best antidotes for overthinking. Through mindfulness, we notice ourselves about to overthink something. Responsibility gently redirects our focus to what we can control, which we get better at doing the skill of meditation.

There is a great practical way to interrupt yourself when you notice yourself about to overthink: just ask yourself 'is this useful?'

Like everything, this is a practice.

How to Reflect—A Few Guidelines

Use a form of reflection that is suited to you.

I simply sit and think. As an ENFJ (the Myers-Briggs classification, which we are getting to in Part 4), I introvert my intuition. This might not be the same for you.

My extroverted intuition friends like to reflect with me through chatting. I know that they need to work things this way.

For some people, writing things down helps them to organise their thinking.

Usually, we reflect because we try to understand something that went wrong or didn't go as expected. That's good. But also use reflection to understand why positive experiences are positive. This is a big clue about your values, which is essential information (and we are looking at this next). It is also a great practice for general happiness and contentment levels, allowing you to savour your experiences and feel grateful. It can anchor you to the present moment.

If you tend to resist reflecting, use questions to help you to reflect. I have included a list of twenty of my favourite self-reflection questions on the next pages.

Combine insights with action. When reflections give you 'aha' moments, find some small way to act on them.

It is possible to use reflection to rewrite the past. This is what can happen in therapy. You rewrite the past when you bring a new perspective to bear what happened.

Solitude as a Way of Bringing Forth Who We Are

I wanted to wrap up with a final, inspiring note about the mysterious role that solitude may play in self-actualisation.

It is from Joseph Campbell's book, *The Power of Myth*. Campbell says having a sacred place (which I am viewing as metaphorical): "is an absolute necessity for anybody today. You must have a room," he says, "or a certain hour or so a day, where you don't know what was in the newspapers that morning, you don't know who your friends are, you don't know what you owe anybody, you don't know what anybody owes you. This is a place where you can simply experience and bring forth what you are and what you might be."

Questions for Self-Reflection

Beginning of the day questions:

- How am I feeling right now?
- How am I feeling about this day ahead?
- What can I accept that I can't change?
- What is it the most important (not urgent) thing that I do?
- What have I agreed to do that I do not want to do?
- Who do I need to be for this day to work?
- What can I do today that will be a unique expression of me?
- How can I be more of 'me' at work and at home?
- What small steps can I take to show that I am serious about loving myself?
- What would scare me slightly that I could do today?

Mindful checks-in throughout the day:

- Where is my attention going right now?

Powerful questions to ask at the close of the day:

- What was the most important thing I did today?
- What gave me the most joy today?
- What caused me the most inner conflict and stress?
- What am I grateful for?
- Do I need to clear anything up?
- What did I learn?
- What do I need to let go?

Powerful questions to ask before you do something big:

- Does it move me towards the boldest, most grand vision I have for myself?
- Will it be fun?

8

The Just Say No Muscle

I stood for nothing, so I fell for everything.

– Katy Perry

Related to learning how to be alone is learning how to say 'no'. No is a complete sentence if you didn't already know.

Without a heightened awareness of your ability to choose what you allow into your world in the form of information, experiences and other people, you will be dictated to by other people's agendas. Also and in my experience, without declining certain demands on your time and attention, you'll wind up feeling resentful and deeply unsatisfied.

What types of things do we want to say no to?

Everything that doesn't add anything meaningful to you and sometimes, also things that do add meaning, but aren't currently a high enough priority in your life. (By the end of this chapter, you should have something to help you to figure out what your priorities are if you don't know already.)

Living an honest life requires steadily getting rid of the irrelevant. Yes, it feels like a sacrifice at first, but only because we are so indoctrinated to value a full schedule over an empty one.

I'd avoid deluding yourself that it is always others derailing you from your worthy goals. The 'just say no' practice involves saying no to someone a lot more devious: the part of you that wants to stay comfortably stuck. In fact, this needs the biggest most defiant no of all.

Why is it So Hard to Say No?

Saying no brings up stuff for people. Some of us have the idea that it is rude or selfish to say no. Others are scared deep down that it equates to a loss in our social standing. And nobody likes to feel like they are letting people down.

There might be a little blowback when we start saying no when people are not used to it. And that is something we have to make our peace with.

However, in my experience, being less available never made anyone less wanted permanently. And sometimes the disdain we are imagining is us projecting our own feelings about being told no.

Whatever your story around no, you can develop freedom from it with awareness.

Saying No to Others

I have found it useful to see saying no to others as an exercise in compassion for them and you. Saying no to people gives them permission to say no.

The author and shame researcher Brene Brown says:

Compassionate people ask for what they need. They say no when they need to, and when they say yes, they mean it. They're compassionate because their boundaries keep them out of resentment.

Dating coach and author Matthew Hussey says that "if we are ruthless in our actions, we never need to be ruthless with our speech." This is a great rule to remember. I have found that delivering 'no's needn't ever be snippy or unpleasant.

It also gets a whole lot easier with our ability to accept no from others. When we are vulnerable enough to ask for what we want when we know we might be denied, the word stops holding such terror.

Saying No to You

So how do we say no to the little immediate gratification monkey? The author Iylana Vanzant pits this struggle as the major one of our lives: "There is no greater battle in life than the battle between the parts of you that want to be healed and the parts of you that are comfortable and content remaining broken."

Saying no to your base impulses is another repeated theme of this book because of its essentialness for self-knowledge. We will revisit this in the Christian Grey muscle.

For now, let's talk about one major way that the lesser self often gets the better of us on a day-to-day level.

Saying No to Technology

I don't want to be a killjoy, but I believe that for most of us, it is helpful to at least consider drastically reducing the daily onslaught and bombardment of information via social media and online news outlets. Unconsciousness is like junk food: in small portions, it is worth pursuing for relaxation, but as a way of life, it leads to extreme passivity. These things are also an absurd attack on your attention span.

Something practical you can do right away is to become notification free. I encourage you to consider, even as a temporary experiment, going notification free and instead checking in at intervals.

I check my phone quite a lot in the day, but it doesn't interrupt me. I go check it when I have got to the end of a thought or a sentence. The pain of completing too many days without making meaningful progress on my tasks is what had me gradually cut down on my usage. I'd never have been able to maintain the focus to write this book, for example, without seriously changing the way I engage with my phone. And never did I once feel that I was genuinely neglecting my friends. I felt guilty sometimes—but that is just a habitual emotional response.

I appreciate that this might not be possible or appropriate for you in your life. I couldn't do it so easily if I had children or ran a business, for example. But most of us can afford to tune down the noise significantly.

You Might Need to Say Yes First

Here is something that I should possibly have stated at the outset: you can't say no without having a clear notion of your priorities, and your priorities are based on your values. In my experience, to know your values, you have to say yes to things and reflect on where it got you. The best experience is often (though not always) garnered through bad judgment.

The writer Beth Kempton says, "Depending on your stage of growth, when you are expanding and exploring, yes is good. When you are refining and honing, no is often better." I have found this to be accurate.

I was never in the habit of thinking about my values before I began exploring personal growth material in my late twenties. Since then, my values have really crystallised before my eyes, and particularly over the last few years as I have said yes to a wider variety of things.

Being able to identify your values is a large source of security. My values help to ground me. They are also what makes decision-making on everything from where I want to travel to who I want to date, relatively easy for me.

How to Figure Out Your Values

To figure out what you value, I suggest using opportunities where you find yourself unhappy or dissatisfied with an experience you brought into your life as an instance from which you can detect a value. Figuring out what you don't stand for can point to what you do stand for.

You can also try a values clarification exercise. To do this, you get a list of values (try the list on the next page) and:

- Start by crossing off the items that are not important to you.

- Then go through the list again, circling as many of the items that are very important to you.
- The remainder of the list would essentially be things that are important, but not very important. Review the very important items. Consider whether there is a value missing that matters a lot to you and hasn't been listed; add it. Then from this group, select seven that are most important.
- Then rank these seven most important values. Number one is the most important value.

For example, here are my seven, more or less:

- Compassion
- Truth
- Learning/growth
- Self-actualisation
- Love
- Family and friendship
- Creativity

List of Values

- Authenticity, Achievement, Adventure, Authority, Autonomy
- Balance, Beauty, Boldness, Belonging
- Compassion, Challenge, Citizenship, Community, Competency, Contribution, Creativity, Curiosity, Collaboration, Change, Communication
- Determination, Decisiveness, Democracy, Diversity
- Equality, Excellence (personal), Excitement, Expertise, Effectiveness

- Fairness, Faith, Fame, Friendship, Freedom, Fun, Family
- Growth
- Happiness, Honesty, Humor, Harmony
- Integrity, Independence, Innovation, Intellectualism
- Justice
- Kindness, Knowledge
- Leadership, Learning, Love, Loyalty, Leisure
- Meaningful Work, Mastery
- Nature
- Openness, Optimism, Order
- Peace, Pleasure, Power, Prestige, Privacy, Productivity
- Quality
- Recognition, Religion, Respect, Responsibility, Relationships
- Security, Self-Respect, Service, Spirituality, Stability, Success, Status, Self-Awareness, Self-realization, Serenity, Self-expression
- Trustworthiness, Truth, Teamwork
- Variety
- Wealth, Wisdom

They say that our underlying values do not change much. I believe that a person's core values are unlikely to be completely different from one life stage to another, but some will be added to the rotation and some taken away. The essential thing is to intend to know what they are and allow them to guide what you say yes and no to.

There is something else that I believe has helped me to know my values.

A Case for Lifestyle Experiments

Ralph Waldo Emerson said, "All life is an experiment. The more experiments you make, the better." I'm with him.

Life experiments are exercises in acting without knowing the answers. They are great for a person who is figuring out what they truly value.

Adding chaos to your life also has the added benefit of training you to do things with no purpose other than that you can. And that stimulates growth and possibilities and new directions in life.

I am a case in point. I wouldn't be writing this book if I hadn't have moved to Thailand when I did. I never wanted to be a writer or a blogger. Those just weren't the kinds of possibilities I was entertaining at the time when my lifestyle was more conventional.

Recall what I mentioned in Part 1 about the force of inertia. Well, experiments are a way of tackling that. They can give you a taste for the opposite.

The opportunities for experimentation are likely to be prolific from wherever you are (and I am going to talk about one we can all do in a moment). Even experiments that seem to be confined to their areas—for example, doing a thirty-day yoga experiment—can spur some quite radical transformations. My own yoga experiment changed my life because of the unforeseen psychological benefits. I believe that my yoga practice has made writing this book possible.

A Scientific Experiment: Minimalism

Minimalism seems to resonate with more and more of us now.

And let's be real, the movement is trendy with those of us who have been privileged enough to have more than enough of what we need.

So does owning lots of stuff get in the way of deepening our self-knowledge?

Chuck Palahniuk, author of *Fight Club*, clearly thought so. He said: "It's only after you lose everything that you're free to do anything."

Personal growth writer Dan Pederson says, "Part of having more, is wanting less. Having fewer wants can greatly uncomplicate your life. It doesn't mean we can't be wealthy (if we have everything we need, we are wealthy). It's about not pursuing wealth as a way of fulfilling yourself spiritually." They are both useful perspectives.

I'm no Marie Kondo, and I'm not going to ask you to throw away your shoes and handbags or ask you to store them a special way. But I will share my belief that there is a link between our number of possessions and our ability to think in a way that is clear and unencumbered.

Not owning lots of stuff is definitely my own preference, but I am not extreme about it.

Methodically going through your stuff and asking yourself what its purpose is in your life can be very illuminating. Particularly the stuff you struggle to let go of.

Marie says the things we love should bring us joy. That's her criteria for keeping them. I believe that we should extend that to the rest of our lives. Everything needs to have a purpose.

Friends and Tribes

The question regarding the people we choose to have in our

lives is an extremely personal one. I'll not intervene or ask you to make sure each of your relationships serves your growth. I don't believe that our friends are here necessarily to serve our growth, although it is definitely a bonus if they do, and they should not be actively destroying it! But for me at this stage, and as I take responsibility for my own growth, I just want to be around those I like, respect and admire.

There is a very popular phrase thrown about on how we are the sum of the five people closest to us. I think it gets misused, but there is some truth in it. Just as we are influenced by what we allow our minds to feed on, of course we are influenced by the company we keep.

Probably the best investment we can make in growing a positive tribe of people is learning to show up more fully as ourselves in our day-to-day lives and engaging in our most loved pastimes. On the practical side of things, doing that tends to mean we will encounter our people in the process of that.

During personal evolution, we grow out of friendships, and that's okay. It is a sad but inevitable part of the natural process of life that we perhaps don't need to struggle against quite so much as we do.

'Where Attention Goes, Energy Flows'

If I had to summarise the importance of the Just Say No muscle in a nutshell, it would be this: where you place your attention is what grows. So start taking your time and attention a bit more seriously.

Get conscious of what you grow with every yes and what you allow to wither with every no.

9

The Roy Walker Muscle

If you're too young to know who Roy Walker is, then I am truly sorry about that.

Roy presented a game show called *Catchphrase* which was very popular (at least in my house) in the 1990s. His catchphrase was: 'Say it like you see it!' And that is what this muscle is about.

It is important to be able to identify feelings as they appear on your radar. And the language available to you affects your ability to do that.

Research about the relationship between words and emotions has shown that learning new words for emotions means you're probably more likely to identify them in your own experience. And the more emotions you can translate from vague things into concrete terms, the happier you'll be.

With greater recognition of our emotions come the following benefits:

- Greater appreciation of how transient emotions are.
- Less likely to fuse with our emotional states.
- A clearer understanding of the potential actions we need to take.

- Greater acceptance of a wide range of emotions in others.

Because of Western values and a few other reasons, mostly our emotional vocabulary is woefully inadequate for the task. This relatively short exploration contains some ideas for improving your ability to accurately decipher emotions.

Finding Your Feelings

The term for giving language to the emotions we observe is 'affect labeling.' You don't need to have an English degree in order to do this. Neither do you need to have been a reader all your life.

But you could read more if you don't already. It's obvious, but your reading habit (or lack thereof) is a big factor influencing the extent of your vocabulary. After a lifetime of reading, we might know how to pin words and sentences to pretty much everything we feel, however ephemeral it might be.

Before I got into the world of non-fiction, I'd read fiction a lot. Stories give us access to a wide range of emotions we have never experienced but one day might. It gives context.

Try to develop a more feelings-based vocabulary by choosing specific content. If you don't usually read books based on human relationships, then give one a try.

Also start talking more about your feelings with your trusted friends. This helps build confidence in communicating your feelings with others.

It's obvious, really, but when you experience an emotion that you don't understand, try to figure out the name for it. To help with this, familiarize yourself with the feelings wheel, Plutchik's

Flower and Parrot's Classification of Emotions (you can find them online).

Finally, consider talks-based therapy. If everyone had the financial means, I am sure we'd all go in for some therapy in our lives. But we can all make some progress in being our own therapists through doing the above things.

When Words Fail Us—The Art of Focusing

Sometimes feelings are slightly out of reach. That's where techniques like focusing can be helpful.

The focusing technique, developed by psychotherapist Eugene Gendlin, allows you to identify your feelings through tuning in to the 'felt sense' of them in your body and suggesting to yourself the possible emotions. The foundational premise is that all emotions and feelings have accompanying physical sensations in the body.

To learn more about how to focus, I recommend reading Gendlin's book, *Focusing*.

10

The #NoFilter Muscle

This muscle is about getting your ego out of the way when you are listening to others and communicating with them.

You might be thinking that the skills of listening and speaking aren't relevant to having self-knowledge.

Well, you're wrong and they are. The way we speak and listen (and not listen) tells us a lot about ourselves.

The Landmark Forum leader Jane Wright said,

We are essentially in conversations with ourselves most of the time—how we listen is determined by our 'concerns' (being successful, being liked, wanting to know 'what's in it' for us, how things will turn out, etc.). That voiceover is not necessarily bad—it's just that we don't really hear the other person, or they us. What we're saying to others, or they to us, might seep in from time to time, but it isn't in what we or they are saying—it's what we're saying plus what they are saying about what we're saying, which isn't what we're saying—vice versa. That dynamic has us miss out on the full possibility of communication—and the infi-nite worlds it makes available.

Ego-less listening and speaking happen naturally in the process of improving your self-awareness. There is one specific tool I would mention to enhance that ability and that is 'non-violent communication'. Read more about it here [artofwellbeing.com/2017/11/24/nonviolent-communication/].

I really recommend everyone to learn the four elements of this powerful self-help process for communication.

Try reading Marshall Rosenberg's book of the same title.

11

The IDK Muscle

What the human being is best at doing is interpreting all new information so that their prior conclusions remain intact.

– Warren Buffett

For the next workout, we return to some further pearls of wisdom from our favourite Greek Socrates, who on yet another good day said: "I know that I am intelligent, because I know that I know nothing." This is 'Socratic ignorance' and it is having an awareness of one's own absence of knowledge. It is the attitude you want to cultivate to know yourself better.

Although it's easy to get them confused, being modest and being humble are not the same. Modesty is the appearance of humility.

An absence of humility can be a person's major stumbling block when it comes to self-knowledge. Mark Twain famously offered: "It ain't what you don't know that gets you into trouble. It's what you know for sure that ain't so."

The more your self-knowledge increases, the more humility you'll have. Flannery O'Connor said: "The first product of self-knowledge is humility." But it's quid pro quo, and you need to have more than a little to begin with. The philosopher and poet David Whyte nailed it when he said that having self-knowledge requires being willing to discard our notions of self at the moment we are presented with conflicting information.

Being humble also serves the process of working on goals. It gives us more of a 'long-game' mentality, enabling us to apply ourselves consistently at our endeavours without being side-tracked by lack of validation.

In Buddhism, to train in staying open and curious—to train in dissolving our assumptions and beliefs—is among the best uses of our human lives. It is awakening *bodhichitta*, nurturing flexibility of mind. It manifests as inquisitiveness, humour; as playfulness.

Below are some suggestions for practices that help to tone the IDK ('I Don't Know') muscle.

Hold Your Beliefs Loosely

Having humility does not equate to being so open your brains fall out (best phrase ever). Nor does it mean we shouldn't have beliefs and convictions. This entire book is made of my beliefs and convictions.

In Part 1, I told you what I thought about your opinions (not much). In thought anatomy, beliefs are more elongated states of being and tend to become subconscious. Joe Dispenza says, "When you add beliefs together, you create a perception. Your perceptions have everything to do with the choices you make, the behaviours you exhibit, the relationships you choose and the realities you create."

The context for what Dispenza is talking about here is how unconscious beliefs can wind up limiting us. Beliefs can have a positive effect too—if you choose positive ones! And yet they are still only beliefs. They are not a fixed part of our identity and should never be treated as such.

I have found it useful to treat my beliefs as in a constant state of flux. This means I am willing to revise my beliefs in light of emerging evidence.

Any time you feel compelled to ardently defend a belief should be a warning sign that there are some underlying fear and insecurity. Passion is okay, but dogma? Not so useful.

We have no need to defend our beliefs or convictions to others. They are there to serve us.

Overcoming Fear of Uncertainty

Those among us who lack humility are those with the most fear in their hearts. When we feel fear, it leads us to do anything to maintain our worldviews.

Therefore, developing greater humility means being okay with uncertainty. The reality red pill practices of mindfulness and responsibility help to overcome a need for certainty, by returning to us our sense of control over the most important thing: our perspective.

Otherwise, overcoming fear of uncertainty is the same as overcoming any other fear: through practicing mindfulness and acceptance. I've made this sound a lot easier than it is. It isn't easy, but it is a practice worth toughing it out for.

Joseph Campbell once said that if the path ahead is clearly

mapped out, it is probably someone else's path. In other words, uncertainty over the future is no bad thing. The hopes and plans we have for ourselves may be nothing compared to the possibilities awaiting us. And we genuinely don't know how things will turn out in life, or if the things we fear are just paper tigers.

There is a Taoist story that is relevant here. It is the story of an old farmer who had worked his crops for many years. One day his horse ran away. Upon hearing the news, his neighbours came to visit.

"Such bad luck," they said sympathetically.

"Maybe," the farmer replied. The next morning the horse returned, bringing with it three other wild horses.

"How wonderful," the neighbours exclaimed.

"Maybe," replied the old man. The following day, his son tried to ride one of the untamed horses, was thrown, and broke his leg. The neighbours again came to offer their sympathy on his misfortune.

"Maybe," answered the farmer. The day after, military officials came to the village to draft young men into the army. Seeing that the son's leg was broken, they passed him by. The neighbours congratulated the farmer on how well things had turned out.

"Maybe," said the farmer.

We could all do with being a bit more like that farmer.

Overcoming Pride

Aside from fear, the feeling of pride is also a big problem for humility. Pride dulls our ability to learn, adapt and be flexible. Pride also makes us sanctimonious and morally righteous. It is particularly a problem in our relationships because it can stop us from apologising or working things out with people. There is an old saying: would you rather be right or happy? It is useful to recall during prideful moments.

Overcoming pride happens the same way we overcome any other self-defeating behaviour: by noticing what we have been doing and committing and recommitting to doing something different.

Having an Awareness of Cognitive Biases

Cognitive biases are ingrained habits of deception. The technical definition is 'a systematic pattern of deviation from norm or rationality in judgment, whereby inferences about other people and situations may be drawn in an illogical fashion. Individuals create their own subjective social reality from their perception of the input.'

In his stark book *You are Not so Smart*, David McRaney says:

> *From the greatest scientist to the most humble artisan, every brain within every body is infested with preconceived notions and patterns of thought that lead it astray without the brain knowing it.*

The only sane way to be less of a victim to cognitive biases is through a mindfulness practice. Early studies have shown that mindfulness helps to counter cognitive biases, including correspondence bias, negativity bias, and self-positivity bias.

Wikipedia has a fantastic comprehensive list of all the cognitive biases. I suggest that you do as I do and save this list [wikipedia.org/wiki/List_of_cognitive_biases] somewhere you can easily reach, and glance over it from time to time.

Being a Student of Something

Being a student is a good way to keep the humility muscles strong. I have always been a student of something. Right now, I am a student of yoga and psychology. I am also, of course, a student of myself and you.

Having a reading habit, which I already spoke about, is a good idea. Readers are naturally more humble in their viewpoints. When you read, and particularly when you read challenging ideas, it forces you to refine your thought. I think that the opportunities for exposure to different ideas and perspectives are difficult to replicate other than with reading.

You can find a list of my favourite books here [artofwellbeing.com/2016/01/22/self-development-books/].

12

The Let it Go Muscle

Apart from the name, there is absolutely nothing Disney about this next muscle.

Humility is letting go of our ideas. But there are other things we need to let go of in order to develop greater self-knowledge and awareness:

- Interpretations of what has happened to us in our lives.
- Attachments.
- Over-identification with our thoughts and emotions.
- Fixed ideas of how the future looks.

This seems to cover a broad range of things, but the common thread is they are all forms of attachment, which you'll hopefully recall from Part 2. Attachment, or identification as it is also known, can be to a story, an emotion or a certain outcome. Our attachments are what cause us to suffer and how we obscure a wider perspective from our view.

But how on earth do we learn to let go of our attachments?

Letting Go of the Past

I'm no therapist. I will just share with you my own limited experience on letting go of painful aspects of the past.

Probably the most painful aspect of my past was my relationship with my mum growing up. I believe I already mentioned that my parents divorced when I was 11. My brothers and I went to live with my mum around the same time I was entering those tricky teenage years. My relationship with my mum rapidly deteriorated and I moved out to my dad's place several times. I felt a lot of anger toward her for what I perceived to be unfair treatment, and I carried that around long after that difficult stage in life was over.

I never considered that my unresolved anger towards my mum would have effects in my life. But of course, nothing in life is isolated, especially when you haven't forgiven someone. I was very independent and never relied on anyone emotionally.

It took a lot of unpacking, but I knew something had shifted in these last few years when my reactions around my mum, which had been on the intolerant side, changed. I was openly loving towards her for what must have been the first time since I was a child.

That happened because I began to see the past a little more clearly. Mostly that she had never been personally attacking me and that I had behaved in ways that would have been genuinely hurtful to her. I came to appreciate her as a person who was always doing the best she could. More and more now, I see only my mum's positive traits (it helps that she has a great many). Importantly I think, I stopped seeing my fraught teenage years as anything regrettable. Instead, I feel thankful for them for helping to shape the woman I am now and who is, most of the time, compassionate to a fault.

Staying angry at someone has a payoff. It can feel good to have it coursing through the veins. But for me, it felt better to be able to be nice, kind and generous with my mum after years of not being able to do that. I secretly hated myself whenever I snapped at her.

I can't tell you 'the one thing' that shifted me into a state of forgiveness with my mum because I think it was a combination of a lot of things. Being with my partner in my late twenties had an overall good effect as did exploring ideas around forgiveness (Iyanla Vanzant and David Hawkins have great perspectives on this—I particularly love Hawkins' book *Letting Go*). Going to Thailand also helped. It was a combination of things all backed by a desire for things to be different—for me to feel different around her. It was slow, but the transformation is now total.

People have bigger things to forgive than this. And it isn't easy. Cheryl Strayed said, "Forgiveness doesn't just sit there like a pretty boy in a bar. Forgiveness is the old fat guy you have to haul up the hill." But you do it for you, not the other person.

I believe that forgiveness happens once we awaken to the gifts of our painful experiences. Actually, I think it might be the key to it.

Letting Go of Attachments

So that's letting go of the past. What about letting go in real time?

Noticing your attachments is simply the first step in gaining freedom from the unpleasant consequences of feeling attached.

The next step is feeling the attraction or aversion whilst maintaining a sense of perspective. Iylana Vanzant says: "The challenge of summer is learning how to enjoy what is present while knowing that it will not last." That's detachment.

Detachment, or non-attachment as it is also known, has its roots in Buddhist philosophy. Detachment as a state is the inevitable consequence when we meditate deeply upon the impermanence of life. Feeling a state of detachment more and more is one of the liberating shifts that a person can experience.

The idea of detachment carries negative connotations. It isn't about retaining a cool, standoffish distance with our love objects and family members. That seems, and I agree, to go against something very ingrained in our hardwiring: the need for love, acceptance and belonging.

But that's not what detachment is. Detachment makes us more capable of love—not less—as it helps you to understand that love springs from within and not without.

There are a lot of books that can help you explore this idea further, and I suggest that you do.

Letting Go of Over-Identification with Thoughts and Emotions

Letting go of our attachment to our thoughts and emotions might be the ultimate in letting go. It can feel like the equivalent of relinquishing our identities. What is identity apart from what we think and how we feel?

Mindfulness trains us in the art of letting go of over-identification with thoughts and emotions. It trains us to witness them, and being able to witness them is a huge step.

One other thing we can attempt to do is to rebalance our intelligences. The theory I am about to elaborate on, a smaller theory within Enneagram Theory (which we are getting to in the next part of the book), is kind of new-ish and there isn't a lot of research on it. I suspect that will change in the future. But given this is the case, I'll keep the exploration relatively short.

Some of us are more identified with our thinking intelligence. More feely types are more identified with theirs and others' emotions. Others still meet the world primarily with a body intelligence which makes them aware of their body sensations and taking action. Theory states that we are all fixated on one of these intelligences which just means that it is our go-to.

- The intelligence of thoughts.
- The intelligence of feelings and emotions.
- The intelligence of our bodies.

Once we are aware of the imbalance in the way we perceive and process our lives, we can seek to integrate the forgotten intelligence. This helps us to become more balanced; reality is less distorted and we are less identified with our ways.

My Story with Intelligences

Despite presenting as a very warm person, I have been a repressed feeler in life. We are fairly easy to spot; we are highly industrious and tend to have a lot of energy, as we aren't being slowed down by our emotions. This person also tends to suffer from the consequences of ignoring the advice of their feelings.

Part of my personal growth has been in giving my feeling

intelligence permission in my life. These days I consciously tune in to how I am feeling and I use that to guide my actions.

Giving our feelings permission is not the same as letting them define your actions. If you use feelings and emotions as a barometer for change, you'll always talk yourself out of it. It is simply about inviting feelings in on the decision-making.

For the other people reading this that tend to consult their feelings last—a key way to use the intelligence of the feelings is just to get out of your head more often (for me, yoga and meditation are key). Practicing gratitude is another good thing to do as this naturally turns the volume up on feelings.

I believe that the subject of reintegrating our lost forms of intelligence offers a great deal of transformation potential for all. But we are in the earliest days of discovering this. The discussion I started here is far from complete.

Letting Go of Plans for our Future

You may be relieved to discover we are back on more solid ground for our next exploration.

Have you ever done an Escape Rooms? They're a lot of fun. If you have never done it, you're thrown into an adventure escape game centre with your mates and in sixty minutes, you need to solve all mystery codes in order to 'break out.'

We approach our lives in the same way as that game. We enter our rooms (lives) and we assume tunnel vision. We are forever trying to get into the next room (living into the future). We scramble around for clues that will get us there; we get excited but then frustrated and disappointed when they seem to lead us nowhere.

But the 'dead ends' aren't a waste of time—we just don't have access to the bigger picture yet. We have to cultivate that big picture thinking ahead of time if we have any hope of making it through.

Joseph Campbell said, "We must be willing to let go of the life we planned so as to have the life that is waiting for us." This is the perfect sound bite for what it means to practice detachment to outcomes.

Detachment to outcomes helped me to write my blog all this time. If I was attached to an outcome—say, getting viral posts—I'd have stopped a long time ago and deprived myself of the learning and meaning that keeping the commitment has given me. In order to evolve into our highest potential, we need the ability to "care and not care" (T.S. Eliot). Detachment has helped me to stay motivated.

The poet John Keats said that 'negative capability'—when "man is capable of being in uncertainties, mysteries and doubts, without any irritable reaching after the fact and reason"—is how Shakespeare created his masterpieces. Put another way, Shakespeare was able to 'subsist in the questions.' We could all do with that ability.

I think Steve Jobs would agree. Jobs told a bunch of graduates once to follow their passions and not worry about connecting the dots. We don't know how things are going to pan out, and so it's better to give up our attachment to results being exactly on our terms.

Summary

Letting go is the most spiritual of all the muscles. These teachings are challenging for a lot of us but also important, as when we let go of who we think we are, we become who we are meant to be.

I hope this chapter has inspired you to consider letting go of some things that don't serve you—whether they are your stories about the past, your fixed idea of how the future will look, or your over-reliance on the interpretations of your thoughts or emotions.

13

The Eye of the Tiger Muscle

Courage is resistance to fear, mastery of fear, not absence of fear.

– Mark Twain

Courage might be the most important personal quality to cultivate given that pretty much anything worth doing in life requires it. Anais Nin said, "Life shrinks or expands in proportion to one's courage," and in my experience, it is really true. And the ability to be consistent has to be a close second.

As the opening quote indicates, naturally courageous people don't have any more bravery than anyone else. They have just learned to manage their fears.

I myself appear as quite a courageous person. I am also quite a fearful person at times, but I tend not to let my fears get the better of me. I believe that we become bold through doing bold acts. And so to develop courage, we all need to do a little (or a lot) of what frightens us from time to time.

What are you the most afraid of? And does that fear stop you from doing what you want to do?

It helps to remember that most fear is a fiction of the mind. When you get good at observing yourself, you won't buy into your stories so much. You'll get good at questioning the fearful thoughts.

Fear is felt in the body, and tuning into the sensations of fear is a great technique for practicing acceptance of fear. You might feel a constriction in your throat, a dryness of mouth. Maybe it goes straight to your belly. Maybe you feel your pulse quicken. You might feel yourself going onto ultra-high alert. Wherever you feel fear, feel it.

Embracing Change

Helen Keller said:

Security is mostly a superstition. It does not exist in nature, nor do the children of men as a whole experience it. Avoiding danger is no safer in the long run than outright exposure. Life is either a daring adventure or nothing.

I love that quote. For me, it says we should learn to value uncertainty a bit more.

Change can be very unsettling, but change is also how we know we are alive. The person that prizes truth above security accepts change as a necessary evil.

There have already been a few occasions during this book

where I asked you to change your values in service of self-knowledge. In Part 2, I asked you to stop valuing pleasure and comfort so highly. In the last muscle, I asked you to stop valuing certainty over uncertainty. Now I am asking you to try to stop valuing safety so highly.

We'll never completely forgo the drive for security; we need to be driven by it sometimes in order to live in this world. But if we can afford to relax that, we must try. I believe this is a natural shift that happens with the practice of responsibility.

Showing Up

The theorist Ken Wilbur says:

One of the core secrets of transformative practice is the enormous impact of intentionally intruding upon and interpreting your comfortable habits. To do so consistently is the secret of keeping your practice alive.

Consistency is what makes our efforts to know ourselves actually bear fruit. It is boring but accurate. If you consistently applied the information in Part 2 of this book, you'd have no need to read the rest of it or any other book on self-knowledge. But the truth about the human condition is that we need to hear the same thing over and over sometimes before we act on it.

There is no magic to awesome outcomes in every sphere of your life. It's all about consistent action over time. Sustained action over time is 'the secret' to long-term success in any endeavour.

Building your ability to be consistent is helped by the practice of the next muscle.

14

The Christian Grey Muscle

The mind is just like a muscle—the more you exercise it, the stronger it gets and the more it can expand.

– Idowu Koyenikan

I've saved the best until last, for this is the gluteus maximus of muscles. That's right: it is the butt of self-knowledge.

The Christian Grey muscle is about developing control over your number one reality processing organ: your mind. And the major practice for that is meditation.

Meditation is a necessity; this is becoming rote. I think (hope) that one day soon, everyone will be at it—on the streets, on trains, in their cars, when at a standstill. Anywhere and everywhere they have a cheeky five minutes.

As I like to recall each time I have the urge to stuff myself silly, our brains evolved during a time when impulse control simply wasn't a coveted thing. We wouldn't live to meet our grandchildren, so we might as well binge on everything in sight and procreate like it's going out of fashion.

The thing is, we will live long enough to bear the consequences of our actions now (hopefully anyway). That is why we need meditation. Well, one of the reasons.

If you have yet to establish a habit of meditating, I would imagine that you aren't clear enough yet on its benefits. The value in meditating is that it helps you to know your mind and master your mind. And this affects everything else, in all spheres of your life. It is how we create the bodies we want. It is how we successfully pursue our goals. Master your mind, and you will do marvelous things. Quite simply, I guarantee it.

If you do not currently meditate, your mind is your master rather than your servant. In other words, your mind is Grey and you are the submissive. For self-knowledge, that has to change.

Although it is inherently wired for lies, your mind is not the enemy. The mind is essentially good, and if you cultivate it, it will blossom.

What Meditation Does: The Four Meditation Superpowers

Before we get to the hows, here are the four meditation superpowers identified by meditation teacher Giovanni Dienstmann:

1. Zooming in—focusing/concentrating.
2. Zooming out—getting perspective/seeing a bigger picture.
3. Pause—refraining from doing a behaviour.
4. Changing channels—switching a line of thought.

Meditation is a lot like what we know of as concentrating.

You are meditating when you notice your mind has wandered, and you return it to the task at hand. In a formal meditation practice, that is simply breathing. But you may begin to realise you can perform most of your activities meditatively. It is certainly what I drew on in writing this book.

The point of meditation isn't to empty the mind. The important part of meditating is the cognitive process of bringing your attention back to your breath. This is what flexes the mental muscles that eventually rewire your brain for the better. Think of it as a mental push up. The more your mind wanders, the more pushups you get to do.

Everyone's mind wanders. Everyone has a monkey up there. There's no such thing as a bad meditator; in fact, if you are dealing with a highly active mind whose attention you need to wrestle back hundreds and hundreds of times, then you get the most practice of anyone.

Dan Harris has a lovely journey to share about meditation that he has written about in his book *10% Happier*, which I have already mentioned. I encourage everyone with any remaining resistance or hang-ups to the practice to read Harris' book. Otherwise, what more is there to say? Meditate until this becomes second nature to you (and it does).

So does meditation always work?

Yes, it does. As Harris says, "There's no magic or mysticism required—it's just exercise. If you do the right amount of reps, certain things will happen, reliably and predictably."

How to Begin to Meditate

You don't need a special cushion, a secret room or half an hour to meditate. Regularity is more important than duration.

Take five minutes anywhere, anytime in your day (although

try to make it the regular place). Sit up straight like your mother told you. Observe your breath. In. Out. As your mind wanders, notice, bring it back to the breath. That is it. Yes, it's less stimulating than checking your email, but it's five minutes dudes. You can do it.

Lots of people I know use the Headspace app to meditate. Give that a try.

Role of Exercise

Mindfulness and meditation are somewhat a slow medicine. It can be a while before you feel like your load has lightened. Exercise, however, is a much more immediate intervention. It is what has kept me sane over the years.

Long before I meditated, exercise was helping me to master my mind and my baser impulses. *Power of Habit* author Charles Duhigg said physical exercise enhances a person's self-control powerfully. If you have been a regular exerciser throughout your life, you will know this already.

One form of movement that I have come to regard as playing a special role in my self-awareness in recent years is yoga. It took me a long time to warm up to yoga—around seven years after I first tried it. The truth is, for a long time my mind was just too hectic to enjoy it. I'd go nuts during a class. I found it a bit slow; it made me feel impatient and irritated.

That all changed in 2016. During my stay in Mexico, I moved into an apartment with an adjoining yoga studio. Finally, I told myself, I will give this yoga thing a shot.

I started to go every day. It began to be the defining feature of my day. I'd get to my mat completely wired with ideas and plans, and by the time I'd roll it up that was all turned down. That is still the way it makes me feel.

One of the reasons my yoga practice has been life changing is because of what I mentioned before about my identification with my thoughts. Practicing yoga has helped that to change. When I get on the mat, I tune out of thinking and begin feeling. It interrupts me in a way that I find completely necessary.

Aside from the physical challenge of it—and yoga can be very physically challenging depending on how you pursue it—practicing yoga has also helped me with the other practices in this book. Acceptance, for example: yoga helps me observe more closely when and what I am not accepting. I can't always see that when I am caught up in life. With the tool of the breath, it helps me to find peace with the challenges of the day. When I leave a yoga class, I feel grateful, inspired, humbled and connected to others. It's like the feeling I only used to get when I was drunk. My personality completely relaxes.

I used a yoga practice to help me to write this book. I don't think it was a coincidence that I found my way to yoga around the time I started writing it. The two were very complimentary. I would spend the first hours of the day working on it and then get to yoga to drop out of my mind. Often, in doing so, the answers to some of the areas of confusion would come as soon as I had relaxed.

But I believe that any exercise can support your self-control and getting control over your mind—just as long as you are regular with it.

Part 4

You've Got a Big Ego (So Does Everyone)

"What's my ego?"

"What you think you want, what you will to believe, what you think you can afford, what you decide to love, what you regard yourself as bound to.

It may be all much too small, in which case it will nail you down."

– Joseph Campbell/Bill Moyers

Time to talk about the big E: your ego.

This book has already made many mentions to the ego or self-construct, so the terms should be a little less alien by now.

Your ego is your most elaborate creation. It includes your unique selection of personal qualities, foibles, insecurities, fears, ambitions and narratives. You may think this sounds like your personality. Your ego and your personality are the same things, really.

But your ego does not define the totality of your being. There's another part of you: a part that is unlimited and waiting to be remembered. It has been buried under a lot of shit. This part has many names (the 'true' or 'essential' nature), but I'm going to refer to it as Z.

Your ego is formed to protect this more innocent part of you early on. When Z just wanted to roam around naked and carefree at school, your ego stepped in and saved you from the embarrassment. It has been doing a similar thing ever since.

This section of the book is dedicated to helping you to flesh out the nature of your own unique ego/self-construct. And strange as it may sound, the purpose of doing that is so you can see what you are not, rather than what you are.

You've already started the work of breaking your over-identification to your image of yourself. This is the role that mindfulness performs—it helps us to identify more with the creator than the created; with the thing that just is, rather than the thing that does.

Each and every time we toggle switch into the Observing Self, we abandon our armour. We step outside of the self-construct. And so practicing mindfulness is how you cultivate egoless-ness in some small way each day. It is how you bring Z back.

This part contains some psychological theory that should help you even more. Before we get to the main observation method, I thought it would be useful to delve deeper into when, why and how the ego was formed.

15

Scoping Out the Self-Construct

Your ego's MO is securing the perception of itself by others and yourself. This is all done in slippery, subtle, covert ways—you aren't conscious you are doing it. As my favourite Brit/Swiss Alain de Botton says, "We are liars of genius. It is part of the human tragedy that we are such natural self-deceivers. Our techniques are multiple and close to invisible."

We develop our egos in order to make it out of childhood alive (more on that in a moment). And our egos are shaped ongoingly by our experiences in adulthood as we are driven to avoid rejection situations and get others' love and approval.

And so it seems there is a legitimate reason why everyone is so obsessed with what happened to them in childhood. Our childhood experiences are instrumental in shaping the people we are now, although we do have more of a choice over that than we realise.

On the Therapist's Sofa

Imagine I'm your therapist, and I've just settled you in my

crusty, dusty but comfy armchair. You're casting your mind back to your childhood where you began developing your 'winning ways' and survival strategies.

American teacher of the personality model the Enneagram (getting to it), Don Richard Riso, says:

In order to master whatever difficulties we encountered [in childhood], we unwittingly mastered a limited repertoire of strategies, self-images, and behaviours that allowed us to cope with and survive in our environment. Each of us, therefore, has become an expert at a particular form of coping which, if used excessively, also becomes the core of the dysfunctional area of our personality.

The logical starting place for a deconstruction of the ego self is the lessons we absorbed in childhood. That is essential work, so if you haven't already, and you are able to get nosy, do so.

What did you do to get parental approval in childhood? What was your major play for avoiding being in their bad books?

There is always logic behind why we are the way we are, and if you want to understand why you do what you do now, you cannot really afford to be a shy historian. Get it done, please. Consider this your first homework for this part of the book.

I think that, given how much a hand our parents had in the way we see the world, it also helps, if possible, to know them as adults. With our adult eyes, we can see where their awareness blind spots may have made their way into ours.

What the Development of the Brain Has to Do With It

This isn't necessary information; I have just found it useful to know.

Also, I'm not a brain expert, so this isn't anything you wouldn't find out yourself with intention and an internet connection.

The brain is commonly represented as divided in two. There is the older, emotional (called the reptilian) brain, which is responsible for our emotions and quick reactions. And there is the newer brain—the neocortex (or the pre-frontal cortex)—which is responsible for conscious reasoning, as well as being home to the personality.

The emotional brain is synonymous with the amygdala, a powerful walnut in the brain which is 'online' from birth. When we talk about the subconscious mind, we are talking about the amygdala's responses, which are swift and often below awareness. This is also the house of intuitive awareness, which you'll recall is information arrived at unconsciously at speed.

The newer brain is rational, sophisticated and conscious of itself, relative to the amygdala's irrationality. Our personalities were traditionally said to be developed by age twenty-five, but psychologists are now saying that we can change after that (if you hadn't figured that out yet).

As our brain encounters life, it is running it by these two main centres. But only the amygdala was around the whole time. It predates the seat of logic. To put it another way, before you had the ability to consciously reason, you ran life through the emotional brain.

Even if we had the most loving and attentive parents in the

world, childhood naturally includes a series of mini devastations. The amygdala is what retains the blueprint of all those. It's like the elephant that never forgets. The emotional brain, determined to keep us safe from threat, hosts limiting ideas about what we are capable of, what parts of us are acceptable and so on.

The problem is that there is no survival threat now, and we don't need protecting. Being identified with our computations of reality, therefore, simply isn't smart. That makes us like children who never left home.

When we continue to view life through the filters of the ego, we are hyper-vigilant against rejection and other failures. When we are exclusively identified with our thoughts and habitual emotional responses, we will feel edgy and insecure. There can be no other result.

Is the Ego Nature or Nurture?

Really, who cares? I've pondered it with the best of them, but we'll never know for sure. All we have are educated guesses.

I had always saddled my horse with nurture. It has taken a big shift in my thinking for me to acknowledge the possibility that our personality traits may follow a set pattern.

At this stage, I believe that is highly likely.

Models for Knowing the Ego

There are several personality models that can assist with observing the ego. I have chosen to discuss with you one main one because I believe that the level of detail it gives distinguishes it as the most helpful. I also briefly mention three additional models that I've found useful to know.

What kind of information can these models help to elucidate?

- Biases inherent in how you compute life.
- How your deepest fears drive your behaviour.
- How to gain mastery over your personality type's weaker points and take full advantage of your strengths.

Before I finally move onto the models, we need to talk about Kevin.

16

WTF is the Hidden Self?

If you shut up truth and bury it under the ground, it will but grow, and gather to itself such explosive power that the day it bursts through it will blow up everything in its way.

– Emile Zola

(Kevin isn't a real person. He is just symbolic of the dark side of your nature. If you've ever seen the movie, *We Need to Talk About Kevin*, or even the Harry Enfield sketch about Kevin the Teenager, the reference will make sense).

The Hidden Self, also called the Shadow Self, is the part that got repressed from your awareness early on in life. It includes unacknowledged desires, personal qualities and emotions. It holds everything we were ever shamed for.

It is important for each of us to uncover and then reintegrate these traits/desires/emotions because what's hidden from our view exerts influence over our behaviour. Carl Jung said: "Until you make the unconscious conscious, it will direct your life and you will call it fate."

There isn't a specific psychological model to use to help you to uncover and reintegrate your Shadow Self back into your awareness. You do it by paying attention. Repressed urges, traits and emotions show up in some way or another in your life. They are begging for recognition from you, and they probably aren't asking nicely.

This section is designed to arm you with a basic method of detecting what thing or things could be a part of your Shadow and to support you in reintegrating them.

How the Shadow Got Formed

Everyone develops a Shadow side during the course of child development.

We may have directly been told that whatever we did/ showed is not ok. Or a behaviour or trait might have provoked a change in treatment, or horror, or an upset reaction from one of our parents. Or we might have hidden the same aspects of ourselves that our parents did.

If you ever spend time with really small humans (I do, as I have three nieces and nephews under four), you'll have the privilege of being witness to a whole self before the division has started. The whole self has no qualms about showing its explosive temper, its uncovered private parts or anything. There is no shame whatsoever! It is a more grown-up version of this wholeness that we are attempting to return to as adults because it is a very non-judgmental and accepting place.

Our parents, who are tasked with integrating us wild, unruly beasts into society, need to show us what's right from wrong. And the less neutral they were about that, the more shame we associate with whatever landed in the wrong pile.

As good parenting models suggest, the trick is in separating the behaviour from the person. When we are told we are wrong for demonstrating natural emotions and qualities, there is an inevitable loss of self-expression. And in order to mentally cope with the conditional love we have been given, our psyche has to split off this part of us and pretend it doesn't exist.

When we deny something in ourselves, we close off that trait to the whole of mankind and become very intolerant of it. And so is born the tendency for psychological projection, one of the psychological defence mechanisms, and the first of our major allies in detecting the Shadow Self.

In addition to projection, there are at least five other ways of discovering and reintegrating Shadow material:

- Peering behind addictions and compulsive behaviour.
- Taking note of feedback from others.
- Noticing envy and infatuation.
- Examining the collective Shadow.
- Peeking behind your strengths.

Becoming Aware of When You're Projecting

We are never angry for the reason we think.

– A Course in Miracles

You've probably heard of the cliché 'if you spot it, you got it.' Or 'what you hate/fear in others, you have it in yourself.'

I first discovered the concept whilst lying on a beach in Turkey during my twenties. My chosen holiday reading, it won't surprise you to know, was a book by Debbie Ford: *The Dark Side of the Light Chasers*. It was a revelation to understand why I'd get so irrationally frustrated with my simultaneously lazy but competent colleague. And why a lady we met on holiday was annoying the crap out of my mum but not me.

A projection is where you notice in others something you have rejected in yourself. It is where you relocate your characteristics onto another. It's quite inventive when you think about it!

Unless we want to stay irritated and disconnected for the rest of our lives, the next step is to reclaim those parts, and see others how they really are. Owning your psychological projections doesn't just improve your self-awareness, it improves your quality of life. It continues to do that for me.

Although there is often a correlation, it's not right to say that whatever virtue/shortcoming you see in others you also have in yourself.

I, for example, always notice inconsiderate behaviour, and I know that that generally isn't a flaw of mine, although I am capable of it sometimes. It is the latter acknowledgement that is key to removing the sting. When people are inconsiderate, it doesn't piss me off to extreme proportions, because I know I do it too at times. When something you notice in others irrationally upsets you, that is a big warning flag pointing to a disowned trait.

Another way to come to identify your disowned aspects is to pay attention to any patterns with the types of characters you encounter in life and your major internal complaints with them.

For me, I just kept encountering needy people and I couldn't see why. It drove me nuts. What I realised was that I have

buried away my vulnerable, emotional side. As I have deliberately sought to let that side show a bit more, others' neediness
has become less of a source of irritation.

It is said that we are attracted towards the experiences and
people that will help the broken parts of us to heal. It's a nice
idea for a self-knowledge devotee.

Looking at Your Addictions

Holding desires in our Shadows, including sexual and creative
desires, can spill out in quite dysfunctional ways for us.

Desire is energy: when we have a desire, it propels us
towards action. If we are holding our finger to the hole, then
that energy has to come out somewhere.

Maybe for you, it will come out in a secret porn addiction.
Or maybe you'll just spend all your time posting and overshar-
ing on Facebook for want of a stronger outlet for your creative self-expression. I think that must have been me as when
I started writing my blog, I virtually stopped posting on social
media. It dramatically lost its appeal.

Of course, not every single dark desire can be acted upon.
Part of being an adult is learning to distinguish the desires
which are going to bring ourselves and others pain from those
that are ok to be given free reign. But our desires need to be
acknowledged at the very least and given a healthy outlet if
possible.

Using Other People

We can learn a lot about ourselves through our interactions
with others, especially people who we can trust to be honest

with us. And we need the inner sustainment to be able to listen to dispiriting feedback along with the positive stuff.

In the end, it is only those who respond to the real us, good or bad, that help us in the long haul. This is people like your family and romantic partners. For a long time, I couldn't take criticism from those I was closest to, as I was too sensitive to it. Since I've taught myself not to feel so threatened by criticism, that has changed.

It takes a lot of humility not to close down in the face of negative feedback. But I would suggest that you change your value around that as I have. Listen to everything, and use some of what you hear to spur reflection.

Our intimate relationships, for various reasons, offer us all the most potential for healing ourselves. Those we are intimate with are capable of pushing buttons that others cannot. When our buttons are pushed, we can run or we can stay open. We have to try more and more to do the second option.

Golden Shadows

I know this sounds like a bizarre sex act you might engage in, but it is actually a reference to our way of hiding positive traits in our shadows as well as negative traits.

So why on earth would we repress positive traits?

We might have needed to play ourselves down for whatever reason not to make others feel bad. Maybe our specific positive traits were simply not valued by our parents. The fact is, we all—every single one of us—forget our own power which is why we are here.

Infatuation, one of the loveliest projections, is a symptom of Golden Shadows. When we're infatuated, we are quite often fascinated and enchanted by the characteristics of another, seeing them as unique.

But as you slowly integrate, that seems to happen less. You still see other people's strengths, but it is less of a 'them or me' deal. You lose interest in idealising or idolising people.

Envy is another big tell on Golden Shadow material. In my twenties, I'd feel envious of confident, powerful, intelligent, attractive women, who I'd have among my closest friends. Privately, I felt insecure that I didn't have what they had. Now that I recognise those qualities in myself, I do not feel envious.

The Collective Shadow

Even if you had the most loving and accepting parents, you still might have stuff in your shadow due to prevailing cultural stereotypes. It's no secret that traditionally, men are oppressed from being emotionally demonstrative. Women can conceal a lot of strength and power in their shadows if they absorbed the message that the point of their existence was to be 'good.'

We can do our bit for everyone's shadows by not succumbing to gender stereotyping in this way in the course of our daily interactions. We can make everything a bit more ok.

It isn't just traits. Emotions like grief, shame, sadness, depression, and anxiety tend to be collectively hushed up. Again, I think a good aim is to create a more accepting environment for these things within our communities and circles.

Peeking Behind Your Strength

Our strengths can signal to our Shadow material. For this exploration, I'll tell you about my Kevin.

My personality strengths are that I am upbeat, resilient and emotionally self-sufficient. That independence, which has served me a lot in life, clues you into a side that we all have that I repressed due to childhood events: a weaker and more vulnerable side.

Reclaiming my forgotten vulnerable child in recent years has improved my capacity for genuine intimacy and connection with people, which is something I really crave. I have learned to be more inter-dependent.

I encourage you to take a close look at what your personal strengths are. Ask yourself if there is anything you can embrace on the other side of that.

Okay—we've discussed Kevin.

Now we can finally move on to the models.

17

How to Use the Enneagram

The Enneagram does not put us in a box. It shows us the box we are already in—and the way out.

— *Don Richard Riso*

The Enneagram, or to give it its full title: the Enneagram of Personality Types, is the personality profiling system that changed my mind about the value of personality models. Learning the Enneagram has shown me the parts of my personality which are habitual. This has changed my life.

I was introduced to the Enneagram, pronounced N-E-O-GRAM, through my friend Rebecca. We met when I was 32 in Playa Del Carmen, where Bex was also temporarily living. We liked each other straight away.

When Bex, who is an ILP (stands for 'Integral Life Practice') coach with deep knowledge of the Enneagram, initially spoke of it, the language seemed alien. There were 'wounds' as well as 'centres of intelligence;' 'basic fears', 'red flags' and 'ways of paying attention'. Frankly, it all seemed a bit gaga to me.

149

But she seemed to be so on point about my motivations and behaviours. That ignited my curiosity a lot and so began my own study of the system.

Background

If you're interested: the Enneagram is a modern synthesis of a number of ancient wisdom traditions, from mystical Judaism, Christianity, Islam, Taoism, Buddhism, and ancient Greek philosophy.

The Enneagram establishes nine specific patterns for how individual human beings lose awareness as the personality or ego self takes its hold over us. This was an initially difficult idea for me to swallow. How could there only be nine forms of madness in the world? I thought I had encountered a higher number than that already. But since learning the Enneagram, I haven't been able to prove it wrong.

The Enneagram shows you how much of what you do and your way of being is mechanical. Enneagram writer and expert Mary Best says: "Each style functions as a mild but profound trance, focussed on a few inward realities that lead to convictions about how the world works and what to do about it." Our problems and the repeated challenges we face are rooted in this trance.

The Enneagram is not vague, which assists us in delving deeper than we have ever been. As Best says: "Generalizations sustain a worldview. Specific observations reveal the illusory worldview and make change easier."

The 9 Personality Types

The nine types that the Enneagram sets out have nicknames:
1. The Reformer.
2. The Helper.
3. The Achiever.
4. The Individualist.
5. The Investigator.
6. The Loyalist.
7. The Enthusiast.
8. The Challenger.
9. The Peacemaker.

Each of the types has a major strategy they use to attempt to meet their needs in life:
1. Be perfect and beyond fault.
2. Be caring and giving.
3. Be successful.
4. Be unique.
5. Be knowledgeable.
6. Be prepared.
7. Be unrelentingly positive and productive.
8. Be strong and powerful.
9. Be easy-going and self-effacing.

Here's some more information, Q&A style, based on some of the questions that have arisen in my own mind on learning the Enneagram and in the process of introducing the system to others.

What is the best way to type myself?

If you aren't fortunate enough to have a trained coach as a friend, do an online test to clue yourself into your type. Your type should be among your top scores.

Then read the fuller description of the types that came out top on the Enneagram Institute website.

A good defining point is each type's deepest fear. If the type you identified really is your true type, then you will resonate with the deepest fear.

WTF? I got high scores in several types!

Consider how the Enneagram is structured and you will see why that isn't unusual.

The Enneagram is depicted diagrammatically as a circle with arrows pointing in all directions. The types are interconnected in various ways.

On a practical level, this just means that you may get scores in your dominant type, your wing (which is your main subtype; one of the types on either side of your dominant type), stress type and integration type. So that's at least four types.

Some common mistypes happen which are explainable when you go into Enneagram theory a bit deeper. For example, types 2 and 7 can look quite similar because they both try to make others happy. There are very different motivations at play though.

Even if the top score isn't your type, your type will be among the top three highest scores, I imagine. Also look for a cluster—look for where you have high scores next to each other.

What should I prioritise knowing about my type?

Once you have identified your dominant type, seek to understand these three aspects:

- The type's passion—the behaviour they do to get their needs met.
- The centre of intelligence of your type.
- Where you currently fall on the line of health/ development (the Enneagram Institute website usefully sets these out under each type's profile).

What are some practical applications of the Enneagram?

Here are some of the main ways I use the Enneagram:

- To improve my awareness of when I am about to do my 'passion', the strategy I use to alleviate uncomfortable feelings. The passion for my type, type 7, is gluttony. Type 7s are driven to want to consume things, experiences and substances in order to feel satisfied. As a strategy, and like all strategies, that has only a limited success. We do better when we gradually stop doing our passions, and our behaviour is more characterised by the virtue on the other side of the passion. In my case, that's sobriety.
- Knowing I am a head centre type, I incorporate my feelings centre a bit more with the intention of addressing the imbalances caused by mostly operating out of the thinking centre.
- I call to mind the healthy characteristics of type 5, my integration point. For me, that has meant slowing

down and staying with my ideas until they are fully developed.

- I am conscious of behaving like an unhealthy type 1, my stress type. This helps me to realise when I am stressed and to self-correct.

I feel like learning the Enneagram has helped me to master the challenges of writing this book—of my type's challenges of doing anything for a large chunk of time without growing despondent.

I believe that using the Enneagram can support all of us in making big and small changes in our lives. It is all about spotting automatic tendencies and recognising that there is a choice there.

Aside from self-knowledge, knowing the Enneagram is a huge empathy builder. I use the Enneagram a lot to improve my ability to relate to others and to see things from their perspective. That has helped me even more with accepting people and not taking their behaviour so personally.

I only want to buy one book on this subject. Which one should I buy?

The Wisdom of the Enneagram by Don Richard Riso.

Is the Enneagram ever not accurate?

Not in my experience. Everyone has a dominant type, and it is evident from their behaviour.

Are there any pitfalls to be aware of?

It may be the most intelligent, informative one out there, but the Enneagram is still a categorization model. Don't learn about your type and use what you learn to limit yourself. That was never the intention of the creators of the model. It was designed to help us to free ourselves, not to limit us further.

The Enneagram theorist Ken Wilbur has said that if the Enneagram is used as an isolated personality system, people can become more identified with their type, rather than evolving. What can help to avoid this is learning/using the Enneagram alongside a vertical system such as the Graves model. The Graves model established levels of worldviews that humans operate from—a sort of values system, if you like. Our worldview (or our 'Graves model profile') dictates the goals we set and the things we care about. You can read more about the Graves model here [artofwellbeing.com/2017/09/05/graves-model].

Beyond that, it is simply a matter of recalling what I mentioned at the start of Part 3—how personality isn't fixed.

18

Other Models: Attachment Theory, Myers-Briggs and Signature Strengths

Okay, so that's the big boy done.

Here are three other personality models I have found useful.

Attachment Theory (Life Area: Relationships)

To my knowledge, Attachment Theory is the most useful theory explaining how we tend to behave in our relationships.

The theory was originally developed by psychologist, John Bowlby, who looked extensively at how children bonded with their parents. Bowlby was able to use that research to set categories for the way we habitually attach to romantic partners as adults, based on that early style. He identified four styles: secure, anxious, avoidant, and disorganised. Each style has its own set of challenges to overcome in the broadly stated goal of connection.

Attachment theory offers us tremendous support to observe unhelpful habits in relationships with others and to create new possibilities for behaving. Amir Levine and Rachel Helle, authors of *Attached* which I really recommend you to read, suggest ways that each style can grow. In particular, the book shows how individuals with anxious or avoidant styles can integrate to a more secure style, thus freeing themselves from much inner turmoil and dissatisfaction.

Read more about Attachment Theory here [artofwellbeing.com/2016/09/02/attachmenttheory]

Myers-Briggs (Life Area: Everything, but Especially Cognitive Functions)

It was only after I finished writing this book that Myers-Briggs wisdom finally landed with me. In the past few months, I have used the system a lot to improve my self-awareness, and it has helped me particularly in understanding how to use my personality strengths.

I really recommend that you check out Personality Hacker's podcast and blog, as their information on making Myers Briggs practical in your life is second to none. What follows is simply an overview.

Myers-Briggs or the Myers-Briggs Type Indicator is probably the most popular personality profiler. It appears to have a lower entry barrier compared with the Enneagram, given that it is a lot less complex. But the fruits of Myers-Briggs come with understanding the cognitive acts of your type.

There are eight cognitive functions in the Myers-Briggs system and each of the 16 types has a different stack (priority system) for how they use them.

Four of the acts help us learn new information, and four help us make decisions. We tend to lead with either learning or decision-making.

Learning processes:

- Introverted intuition – 'Perspectives'
- Extroverted intuition – 'Exploration'
- Introverted sensing – 'Memory'
- Extroverted sensing – 'Sensation'

Decision-making processes:

- Introverted thinking – 'Accuracy'
- Extroverted thinking –'Effectiveness'
- Introverted feeling – 'Authenticity'
- Extroverted feeling – 'Harmony'

Your primary cognitive processes together should paint an accurate portrait of your strengths.

My Myers-Briggs classification is ENFJ. The cognitive acts for ENFJ are:

- Leading: Extroverted feeling – connecting and considering others and the group.
- Supporting: Introverted intuiting – foreseeing implications, transformations, and likely effects.
- Relief: Extroverted sensing – experiencing and acting in the immediate context.
- Aspirational: Introverted thinking – analyzing, categorizing, and evaluating according to principles.

There are various theories on how best to use this information for personal growth. I am aligned with Personality Hacker's theory that growth happens in the awakening of the supporting cognitive function, which for me is 'introverted intuition'.

This book isn't the time and place for a deep dive into Myers Briggs, although maybe for the next one. If you are unfamiliar with Myers Briggs, I encourage you to do the personality hacker online test to discover your Myers-Briggs style and then familiarise yourself with the cognitive acts for your type. Start there and you can always deepen the exploration as and when.

Signature Strengths

Signature strengths is a classification model developed by psychologist Martin Seligman that helps you to understand your main character strengths. The VIA Classification of Character Strengths is comprised of 24 character strengths that fall under six broad virtue categories: wisdom, courage, humanity, justice, temperance and transcendence. They are morally and universally valued, encompass our capacities for helping ourselves and others and produce positive effects when we express them.

Seligman found that the more we draw on our signature strengths in our work and lives, the more meaningful our life will feel to us. In fact, if we can redesign our lives around using these strengths, we will feel immensely satisfied and as if we are tapping the most essential positive parts of ourselves to contribute to the world. We will be living the good life rather than the simply pleasant life most of us live.

Seligman said: "The 'pleasant life' might be had by drinking champagne and driving a Porsche, but not the good life. Rather, the good life is using your signature strengths every day to produce authentic happiness and abundant gratification. This is something you can do in the main realms of your life."

A list of all 24 of the strengths is available here [viacharacter.org/www/portals/0/graphic2014.pdf].

Summary

Coming to know your ego isn't an easy task. But it is absolutely worthwhile. Knowing the cage that we tend to see life out of helps us to break free of its confines.

An ego-led life has been described as a life of 'low-grade crisis' where we are always reaching and never arriving.

Okay, we made it through the rocky patch.

Now let's look at a few of the states that await the person who has chipped off some of the marble.

Part 5

The Real Slim Shady

In the final analysis, we count for something only because of the essential we embody, and if we do not embody that, life is wasted.

– Carl Jung

'I am' is a complete sentence. It has taken me so long to appreciate that.

I am Rezzan, true, but that is just my name.

I am an editor, a writer, a website owner, a person that practices yoga. But these are just the things I do with my time.

I am an 'ENFJ' and an 'Enthusiast.' But these are maps, not the territory.

I am a sister, daughter, aunt, friend and sometimes girlfriend. But these are just some descriptions of how I currently relate to others.

I am productive, I am smart and I can be really fun. I'm lazy, selfish—selfless. I am all of these things and much, much more.

I am limitless.

I am. It's a complete sentence.

I think that being in a state of expanded awareness, instead of being so 'in the grip' of our personalities, is one of the best shifts that happen in life. I think we are here to remember who we really are, before we slipped into the trances and the strategies that define us.

And we are all giants —every single one of us. We are all the elephants being held back by the tiny strings. First we may experience that only fleetingly, but with practice, more and more.

Those that have attained a 'higher state of consciousness' become quite child-like. Picture the Dalai Lama. The guy seems so uncomplex and unaffected, perhaps even simple. But I think that joy flows from a deep understanding of the nature of the self.

Although the process is called 'self-discovery,' the true nature isn't discovered but gradually remembered. Our true selves emerge from the process of unlearning the junk that we cover them with. And it becomes clear what we really want to do.

I didn't go hunting for purpose, or creativity, or any of the states that I am going to talk about in this part. They came to me as I started to pay attention differently to myself and life.

What follows isn't a scientific list of things we can all expect upon greater self-awareness. But it isn't some bullshit list of things either.

These are states I never thought I could say characterise me, but now all of them do and a lot of the time, because of the practices I have been telling you about in this book.

19

The Emerging States of Self-Knowledge

- Joyful.
- Grateful.
- Purposeful.
- Creative.
- Genius.
- Light-hearted.
- Trusting.
- Patient.
- Motivated.
- Loving and connected to others.

You've probably felt all the above at least once in your life, if not more. But in my experience, enjoying them in a longer-lasting way only comes from consistent reality red pill application.

Some of the states may be reverse engineered to produce a higher state of awareness. The media has done a phenomenal job of glamorizing gratitude, and now many people are using a gratitude practice to experience states of egoless bliss in their days, which is great.

But the pull to self-deception is strong, and when the fog descends, we need to go back to basics:

- Am I paying attention non-judgmentally on purpose?
- Am I controlling my perspective and actions?
- Is my awareness inclusive of all my thoughts and feelings?
- What is my ego having me do?

With practice, I find that the emerging states are more pronounced in life.

The descriptions below are offered as short thought pills rather than being instructional, which reflects my belief that we simply need to awaken to these things by paying attention in our new ways.

Joy

Joy—the feeling of great pleasure and happiness—can happen aside from through knowing and understanding. I felt joy last night when I was singing karaoke!

But in my experience, joy only becomes a lasting state when you develop a deep understanding of your true nature. Only then does your baseline happiness improve.

As I said in the beginning, I have found myself to be surprisingly joyful now that I am less in the way of myself. It has taken time, but it's there. I feel like a smile or a laugh is never far away. And maybe a large part of that is I don't clutch onto happiness like I used to.

Gratitude

A grateful mindset is an extremely powerful one. I believe there are studies showing that practicing gratitude literally changes the mind, helping to rewire it away from the default states of negativity. We should all be practicing gratitude proactively, and definitely on the days where finding a positive frame of mind is more challenging.

You'll naturally feel more grateful once you are practicing mindfulness, acceptance and responsibility. As we awaken to the illusions we are under, we struggle to stay ungrateful. That's because presented with the truth of our lives, feeling grateful is irrepressible.

There is a funny thing about gratitude. The more grateful a person becomes, the more that life seems to give you things to be grateful for. It is a mysterious natural law that I can't account for but have experienced. Gratitude is correctly called 'the ultimate state of receiving.'

And if we go onto entitled mode, or we are struggling to accept (which will happen at times), we can use a gratitude practice to reset us emotionally or jolt us out of that. The author Neal Donald Walsh said, "Gratitude reverses any idea that something that is going on should not be happening. And then, we have found peace."

I've written about how to develop a pervasively grateful mindset here [artofwellbeing.com/2017/12/15/gratitude/].

Clarity of Purpose

Having clarity of purpose is quite a big deal. It makes every day meaningful when you feel that level of connection to what you are doing and how you are passing the time.

We feel the most purposeful when we learn to wield our key strengths in the service of a cause, usually involving others. Doing so takes effort, but organising your life around your core desired feelings and values is a life of meaning.

I was thinking as I was writing this section about parenthood. I'm not a parent myself, but I have observed that parenthood seems to give people a huge sense of purpose. Perhaps this is because of the huge service element and because the evidence of your impact is so clear.

One of my favourite experiences of recent years has been watching the process of my brothers and best friend become parents and seeing them step up to the task. It seems like the ultimate in personal growth and automatically quieting to the ego.

Not everyone wishes to be a parent. In the happiest lives, we can get a sense of purpose from a cross selection of our pastimes in our personal lives. I like the psychologist Ernst Becker's idea that purpose is how conscious we are of what we are doing to earn a feeling of heroism. Maybe we all secretly want to save the world in the way that only we can.

And as we already looked at, one key source of fulfillment in life has to be our work. I think we all ideally want to derive a sense of purpose from the work we do. It doesn't need to be anything that special: just as long as we feel we are using our qualities to advance the human cause, or in some way be of service. There must be a hundred ways that can transpire for each of us.

As to what that thing or things are—we have to all find out.

In his book *The War of Art*, Steven Pressfield states:

We're not born with unlimited choices. We can't be any-thing we want to be. We come into this world with a specific personal destiny. We have a job to do, a calling to enact, a self to become. We are who we are from the cradle and we're stuck with it. Our job in this lifetime is not to shape ourselves into some ideal we imagine we ought to be, but find out who we are and become it.

I believe that a person can let purpose find its way to them by paying attention to the things that engage them the most. As we begin to construct our lives in a way that is more in keeping with our own values, it is likely we will gravitate towards the types of work that use our unique combination of skills. We will notice opportunities to do that and we will act on them.

My Story with Purpose

It makes me a little sad to say this, but during my twenties, I had no conception of what value I was offering to the world. Not just in my work, in my whole life. I wasn't aware of my impact on others at all.

When I began exploring ideas around purpose, I'd feel hopeless and despondent. I could do so many things to an average level, but nothing really stuck out.

But there are aspects of brilliance in each and every one of us. And finding those jewels involves paying close attention to your curiosities and passions as well as noticing what other people say about you and how they rely on you.

Sometimes, you just have to try a lot of things and see what sticks. For me, and because I had drifted so far from my natural enthusiasms, that's how I reconnected with the pastimes I derive meaning from.

Before life got serious, I had loved English literature. But at the point I did my undergraduate degree in law, my natural passions got placed on hold. I just forgot about them, getting caught up in University and then working life.

I cannot regret my legal training or experience as it challenged me to grow some of my weaker faculties. But I never loved anything like I loved analysing the truths being told through the characters in my beloved books, and the universal themes being presented through plotlines.

Starting my blog probably marked my first step into using my natural enthusiasms as a way to attempt to serve others. Writing this book has also felt deeply purposeful for me.

But I also get a sense of purpose on many other occasions. I feel it the most when I am supporting and encouraging others, which I suppose is why I tend to gravitate towards those who will be open with me and share their thinking and feeling. I guess I am taking a wider construction on purpose than I used to.

Just because you're successful at something doesn't mean it will bring you purpose. A person can excel without ever feeling like what they are doing matters in a deep way. In his book *The Big Leap*, the author Gay Hendrix describes this as being in your 'realm of excellence,' but not in your 'realm of genius.' In our realms of genius, we are using what's inside us to change the external world in some small way.

Creativity

How creative you are isn't determined by your profession. The writer William Plomer said creativity is the power to connect the seemingly unconnected. This is how I tend to view creativity these days.

This capacity for creative thought is a state we all possess. It is a state that helps to negate the uncertainty of life. Although some of us are naturally more inclined to lead with this capacity, we all have it, and as we become more whole, it is characteristic in each of us.

I also think that we all have a reserve of creative energy—a desire to make or build. My creative energy these days goes into writing, but not always so. I used to enjoy being creative with my clothes. In my twenties, I was creative with food in a big way. I like to think of creativity as being unlimited because that makes me feel the most liberated.

In my observations, the happiest people have a regular outlet for their creative energy. I think that without a creative outlet, creative energy becomes stuck and manifests as low-level addictions and compulsions and frustrations. For me, a dormant creative desire was a source of a wordless sadness and frustration I felt at times. When I began writing, a reservoir of previously untapped well-being opened up for me.

The anathema to both creative energy and thought is allowing other people's values to dictate our lives. That's why for a lot of us, creativity gets lost in the process of growing up and having responsibilities. But the more we practice the things in this book, the more of our creative potential is restored to us.

Feeling inspired—a sense of wonder and awe—is another symptom state of awareness. The opportunities for wonder and awe are prolific and we obscure them with the way we pay attention.

Some of us are called upon to use our inspiration to make art. And the best artists know that they needn't wait passively for inspiration to strike. Top creatives all say that the secret is in maintaining a certain state through the use of structure and routines. And when you go deeper into their methods, you can see that they are carefully managing their attention in the same ways we have looked at.

Genius

Genius is the ability to put into effect what is in your mind. There is no other definition of it.

— *Scott Fitzgerald*

I believe that talent is just a lot of showing up repeatedly for the things we love and are curious about. In other words, I believe it is cultivable. And our stamina for practice sustains itself on love, not a desire for money or success. And so ultimately, talent and genius are derived from innate interest.

When you dig into the lives of those that are widely recognised for genius (read Robert Greene's book, *Mastery*), you can see among the geniuses the evidence of a healthily narcissistic preoccupation with their curiosities from an early age.

The writer Alain De Botton (clearly a genius) says:

*Genius can in this sense be defined as paying closer atten-
tion to our real thoughts and feelings and being brave and
tenacious enough to hold onto them even when they find
no immediate echo in the world beyond. We operate with
a false picture of genius when we identify it too strongly
with what is exotic and utterly beyond us. It is something
far more provocative than this.*

Joseph Campbell said it even more simply: 'follow your bliss.'
Give it a try—it might take you all the way to genius.

Motivation

The mystic Edgar Case says that all of us have an unlimited
supply of motivation within us—it is just a question of align-
ment with what matters to us. If you believe that to be true (I
do), then motivation does emerge from the process of knowing
yourself.

Motivation is inherent and self-knowledge gets the crap out
of its way. It gets rid of the inauthentic goals and the low self-
belief. It kicks procrastination to the curb.

A person can be driven by an ego agenda and appear very
motivated. I've been motivated my whole life, never really suffering from laziness. But I wasn't always so much pulled by my
values, as just addicted to feeling productive. I was busy for the
sake of filling the void.

I have found that the feeling of motivation does wax and
wane a little, but it is consistent now I work more on things

that I feel aligned with, and I have greater impulse control. This feels like authentic motivation to me.

Lightness

A person's playfulness, provided it isn't a forced characteristic, is evidence of a high degree of self-knowledge and awareness. In fact, if we were self-knowing, we'd have no option but to lighten up and stop taking ourselves so seriously.

I've always been an upbeat sort of character, but my good cheer has in the past been a little forced at times. I've always felt like I need to keep the mood up.

And I still have the urge to play the clown with my friends. But I also feel genuinely light-hearted pretty much all of the time. I attribute that to dropping some of the baggage in the form of negative thinking and limiting beliefs.

As for actually playing—well, all adults should indulge in that, if only as a route to stay connected with our inner children. Play relaxes us, puts things into perspective, and it is what enables that all-important creative state.

We all play in different ways. I feel like I'm playing at yoga—it reminds me of when I was a kid and used to go to gymnastics. I play a lot on my blog with ideas.

How do you play?

Trust

For me, trusting others has never been a huge issue. I tend toward trusting people.

Trusting myself has been a different matter and I think it comes right back to living in my head all the time. I believe that feeling trust in life is hard for any 'head types'—overthinkers and rationalisers.

These days I feel much safer in the guidance of my own feelings, intuition and judgment. I trust myself more than I trust anyone.

Patience

I was never naturally patient. But patience has been the by-product of self-knowledge for me. I have found that I don't need to have everything I desire immediately. I can enjoy what I do have whilst working on the things I want. I have a lot more grace now and I am a lot less controlling.

When you have developed patience, time becomes sort of your friend, and so you stop fearing the passage of time quite so much. I don't pretend that I have all the time in the world (that's crazy) but because I mostly use the time on what matters to me, time is no longer my enemy.

Love and Connection

Love is paying attention. It really is.

For me now, and because of the changes I made in how I pay attention, love for others comes relatively easily. Yep, even when I am sleep deprived and/or starving! Even then, you'll find me relatively generous-spirited.

Being able to love other people can only happen once you love yourself. And the practices in this book naturally cause you to love yourself more.

I was at a talk being given by the meditation teacher Sharon Salzberg recently where she was on tour promoting her new book about love. Sharon described love as an ability, not a state. Yes, I thought. Later, I shared this definition with my mum and she scoffed and dismissed it out of hand which didn't actually annoy me (much). I totally got it.

We are so used to thinking of love as a feeling. As I indicated, my experience of love and my views about love have changed a lot in the process of self-discovery. I no longer see real love exclusively as a feeling but as a capacity that arises naturally once we loosen our defences and destructive patterns of behaviour.

The good thing about seeing love as an inherent ability is that the experience of love becomes an internally generated state. Sounds lofty, but it happens.

You also begin to see everyone as your potential benefactor and beneficiary. I do not feel like loving behaviour is reserved for only the people whom I share my life with. I exercise my ability to love freely and with everyone I can. I'm a total hussy with it!

20

Wider Benefits of Self-Discovery

Although it is rarely a motivating factor (at least initially), developing self-knowledge is the most effective contribution we can make to others and to changing this world.

The author Stephen Cope says, "The world doesn't need more people offering what they think the world needs. The world needs more people awakened to what they want to do."

It seems a little extreme to say it, but unless and until we are engaged in deepening our awareness of ourselves, we are basically a violent person. Not violent in the traditional sense of the word perhaps, but violent with the extent of our unconscious behaviour.

We take out our stresses on others. We do jobs that aren't befitting of our skills, therefore, depriving the world of them.

In her book *Heart Advice for Difficult Times*, author Pema Chodron says:

Times are difficult globally; awakening is no longer a lux-

ury or an ideal. It's becoming critical. We don't need to add more depression, more discouragement, or more anger to what's already here. It's becoming essential that we learn how to relate more sanely with difficult times. The earth seems to be beseeching us to connect with joy and discover our innermost essence. This is the best way we can benefit others.

Self-knowledge makes us more compassionate. And the world is crying out for that.

Epilogue

Self-knowledge has no end—you don't come to an achievement, you don't come to a conclusion. It is an endless river.

— *Krishnamurti*

Working on this book has given me a lot.

It has given me a certain purpose when I listen to people. And it has incentivised me to use my time in the wisest and—as it emerged—most satisfying way possible. I don't think this has made me the most endearing company for the last twelve months. But, as they say, everything is a trade-off.

I have found that the private awareness of selecting and committing to this path has been a huge reward of itself. I think that is what any good goal does: it drip-feeds us fulfillment through all of the phases, from idea to fruition.

And of course, I had a few darker days. A scary goal will bring up all of your internal resistance in the form of beliefs, thoughts, feelings and self-sabotaging behaviours. Writing this book lived up to that. One regular and destructive line of thinking was:

Who am I to write a self-help book, when I continue to behave so cluelessly at times?

But you have to love yourself through the fat/ugly days and through shitty early drafts. You have to hold yourself through the process of dying off bad habits and establishing new ones.

It's all too easy to fall into the trap of hating where we currently are. But those times of impatience are opportunities to practice acceptance and compassion. When you can do that, you've found a level of freedom that most people never reach.

With self-discovery, the work is never complete. Thomas Jefferson said: "The price of freedom is eternal vigilance." He must have been talking about this process.

You might have learned some things from this book, which is great. But let it be the start or the continuation of your self-discovery journey. Don't do what I used to do and just read interesting books, say 'that's nice' and forget about it. Tony Robbins says never leave the scene of an idea without implementing some action. Someone else said if you want to see different results in life—do something different.

My Note from the Universe said today, "It's not the size of your dreams, REZZAN, that determines whether or not they come true, but the size of the actions you take that implies their inevitable arrival."

Pull your finger out, basically.

So here we are, at the end of the book. I hope that you have learned some things that serve your self-awareness and ultimately, your happiness.

Perhaps the most important message of this book is simply this: the answers to your happiness and wellbeing do not lie outside of yourself. You can become your own guru as I have: by changing the way you pay attention.

And by not giving up on yourself. Never.

Not ever.

About the Author

Rezzan is an editor by profession, and she teaches self-empowerment at her blog, *Art of Wellbeing* at artofwellbeing.com. A trained coach, Rezzan started writing and blogging when she traded in her 9-5 lifestyle for a more irregular lifestyle of travel. For the past three years, she's lived everywhere from Thailand to Mexico. She wrote her first book off the back of that experience, having discovered what she thinks is the answer to lifelong happiness—knowing yourself. Find her on Twitter @artofwb1, on Facebook at facebook.com/rezzanartofwellbeing.

YOU MIGHT ALSO LIKE:

101 Essays That Will Change The Way You Think
by Brianna Wiest

This Is For The Women Who Don't Give A Fuck
by Janne Robinson

What I Didn't Post On Instagram
edited by Chrissy Stockton

Thought Catalog Books is a publishing house owned by The Thought & Expression Company, an independent media group based in Brooklyn, NY. Founded in 2010, we are committed to facilitating thought and expression. We exist to help people become better communicators and listeners in order to engender a more exciting, attentive, and imaginative world.

Visit us on the web at
www.thoughtcatalogbooks.com and *www.collective.world.*

Made in the USA
Lexington, KY
08 June 2019